D1075107

God In Us

God In Us

*A Liberal Christian Philosophy of Religion
for the General Reader*

◇◇◇◇◇◇◇◇◇◇◇◇◇◇◇◇◇◇◇◇◇◇◇◇◇◇◇◇◇◇◇◇◇◇◇◇◇◇

By

A. CAMPBELL GARNETT
The University of Wisconsin

WILLETT, CLARK & COMPANY

CHICAGO   NEW YORK

1945

MGE

To

CORPORAL JOHN M. GARNETT

Contents

Contents

Preface

THIS BOOK has been written in response to a number of requests from readers and reviewers of my previous work, *A Realistic Philosophy of Religion* (Willett, Clark & Company, Chicago, 1942). Its purpose is, first, to present the liberal Christian philosophy of the earlier work in a way that can be readily understood by the ordinary educated young person without the assistance of a teacher. Second, to discuss from the same point of view a number of questions only lightly touched upon in the earlier work, such as revelation, sin and salvation, the nature of Christ, Christian institutions, prayer, miracles, and the argument from design. Readers of the former book will find some of the same things freshly and more simply stated, but most of the subject matter is entirely new.

To achieve simplicity I have abandoned dialectic. In writing for students of philosophy it is necessary to state and criticize many alternative theories. This makes very difficult reading for those not familiar with the views discussed. In this book, therefore, I have reduced this type of argument to a minimum. I have, instead, gone straight to the relevant facts, stated the questions they raise, and then proceeded to draw from them the interpretation they seem most consistently to suggest. Those who wish to pursue the subject into critical dialectic I would ask to read my two earlier works in this field, *A Realistic Philosophy of Religion* (1942) and (still more metaphysical) *Reality and Value* (1937).

Liberal Christianity has for fifty years or more been seeking solid ground whereon to set its feet. The thesis here presented claims to have found such solid ground by showing that the disinterested will to the good of others is the activity of God within us. At the same time it claims to preserve the essential truths which have made Christianity a power for the salvation of the individual and society. As such it refutes the charges of the old and the new orthodoxies while admitting much that is of importance in their insights, especially those of the latter. It also rejects the negations of the humanists and agnostics, though adapting itself to what seems valid in their critique of the religious tradition. It presents a philosophy and theology that claim to be true to the scientific knowledge of our day and to the deepest historic insights into man's religious experience. It rejects and reinterprets much of traditional Christian theology but claims that the new interpretation is more true to the spirit and thought of Christ. It proceeds by the methods and in the spirit of liberal Protestantism, but recognizes the errors in that tradition and returns to find deep elements of truth in much that it has frequently discarded.

In a field where so many have labored it seems like an impertinence to claim to say something that is fresh and true. But what seems fresh and true to the author may seem so to others. At least it contributes its quota to that never ending labor of thought whereby truth is found and maintained.

A. CAMPBELL GARNETT

The University of Wisconsin
Madison, Wisconsin

God In Us

Have We Outgrown Religion?

IS RELIGION WISHFUL THINKING?

O N THE DAY I first sat down to plan the outline of this book, a report came over the radio that all the taverns in a neighboring town had closed, and the tavern keepers had posted notices in their windows advising their patrons to go to their churches and pray. No! It was not that the tavern keepers had all been suddenly converted to prohibition. It was Invasion Day. That morning our boys had stormed the beaches of Normandy. Thousands had died. All were in peril. The war had reached its hour of crisis. The action of the tavern keepers was simply a fine gesture, in an unexpected quarter, that expressed the mood of the nation. Throughout the United States and the British commonwealth the same impulse was manifest. The President gave to the world a prayer he had written in the night, before the rest of us were aware of the news. The British king called on his people all round the world to pray. Everywhere the churches were opened and throngs entered them for prayer.

Such a demonstration makes it plain that we have not outgrown our religion. Many of us habitually neglect it. But few of us have entirely given it up. Yet there are some who very persistently say that we *ought* to give it up. And many more, especially among those who habitually neglect it, wonder whether they are right. A religion that a person does not practice, except under emotional impulse in times of danger or distress, is not very convincing to anybody. It is easy to compare it to a mere superstition, which a man rationally ignores in his ordinary affairs but turns to as a last resort in his difficulties or relapses into in moments of emotional distress. It suggests that the belief in God is merely a product of wishful thinking, something that people try to believe in because it is a comfort in times of trouble to think of an omnipotent helper, and a consolation in face of disappointment and death to think of an eternal reward in an afterlife.

Perhaps there are some people who believe in God simply for the comfort they get out of it. But there are also a great many people who doubt or disbelieve in God because of the discomfort they have found in the idea. The traditional and orthodox picture of God is not a very comforting one. The modern tendency to believe that God is so full of love and mercy that we can neglect him, ignore his will, follow our own selfish desires entirely, and still turn to him for help in time of need, is in large part a product of wishful thinking. But this is not the traditional picture of God. In that picture God loves his children, but makes very difficult demands of them. He is full of mercy, but he is just. He rewards and he punishes. He is able and willing to save. But the way of salvation calls for discipline. The further we go back in history the more do we find the emphasis on discipline.

Whatever may be true of some modern modifications, man's original belief in God was not a product of wishful thinking. God was primarily one to be feared. Christianity taught that those who honor and trust him

find him one to be loved. But the Father who receives
the prodigal is still the source and upholder of the moral
law. And who among us is not conscious of having broken the moral law? Thus wishful thinking is more often
a cause of unbelief than of belief in God.

GOOD AND BAD RELIGION

The sort of religion that manifests itself only in appeals to God for help is but a weak remnant of a faith
which arose because men believed that the moral law is
rooted in a will that is greater than their own, and that
the moral law is good, an instrument of love. The religion that is practiced only in foxholes is a poor surviving
fragment of a faith that inspired our fathers to demand
from kings and tyrants the recognition of the equal rights
of every man to think for himself, to speak his thoughts,
and to have his person respected before the law. That
religion gave them courage to fight for freedom because
they believed that freedom was a law of God, above the
laws made by men. Before that God they bowed in humility and fear. And yet they trusted in his justice and
love. He was no product of wishful thinking. Wishful
thinking may rob a man of his religion. It may drain
the power from it by soft-pedaling the moral element and
leaving only a Santa Claus who brings us gifts. But it is
not the original source or chief sustainer of belief in God.

If on D-Day people prayed who had long neglected
prayer, if men have prayed in foxholes who never prayed
before, it was not because their anxious wishes created
faith or strengthened it. It was because they had long
retained in the back of their minds a belief in a rule of
right and wrong that is above the desires of men, and in
a Power who upholds that rule and who therefore is just

and good. They may often have failed to follow his rule, but they still believed in his goodness and in some possibility of his power to help them. And so they prayed. The prayer was a natural expression of a faith that rested on something much deeper than their wishes.

But if it was merely a prayer for help in a physical difficulty, divorced from all consideration of right and wrong, it was illogical and unworthy. It ignored the deeper basis of faith, the conviction that the moral order derives from an authority that is more than human. It tried to avail itself of God's love without thought of his righteousness. And an appeal to love without thought of righteousness is an appeal for favoritism. It is a relapse to the primitive man and the pagan, who think of a god who specially rules and guards his chosen tribe, or a god who can be bribed with promises and offerings to work miracles in the special interest of individuals.

If those who say we ought to have outgrown religion meant merely that we ought to have outgrown such primitive and spasmodic expressions of it they would be right. But they mean much more than that. They mean that we ought to have outgrown the conception that there is any source or support of the moral law above the desires of human beings. They believe that modern science has undermined all ground for belief in any being higher than man, to whom we may look for guidance and aid, either in things spiritual or in things material. They tell us that religion, even at its best, is merely a survival of ancient superstitions, a hankering after unattainable blessings, a reverence of nonexistent authority. They usually fail to recognize the strength it brings to the moral life. Or if they recognize this they charge that it is too dearly bought at the price of rigid adherence to outworn codes, opposition to freedom of thought, and waste of effort on futile ceremonies.

These charges against religion are not without foundation. But they go too far. They throw out the wheat with the chaff. What our religion needs is not a tornado to blow it away, but a winnower to sift it. It is true that science has shown many religious ideas and arguments to be untenable. It is true that religious thought harbors still some superstitions of a bygone age, that it sometimes imposes outmoded restrictions, opposes freedom and wastes effort. So does every other human institution. The congress, the law courts, the economic system and the army must be constantly overhauled and revised to incorporate new knowledge and adapt them to new conditions. So must our religious beliefs and practices.

There is a core of permanent truth and value in all these things. But it has to be related to factors which are constantly changing and only half understood. Sometimes it becomes almost lost under an accumulation of these extraneous factors. Then we need a revolution or a reformation. But the revolt ends in disaster unless it succeeds in recovering and reinstating the core of truth and value. That is what we need to do today with our religion. This book is an attempt to winnow the wheat from the chaff, and to show that it is real wheat.

RELIGION AND SOCIAL ORDER

Every human society has its religion. And everywhere religion performs the same essential function. It is the cement that binds the society together. It upholds the social structure. This is the statement of Dr. R. R. Marett, of Oxford, one of our greatest living anthropologists. This idea is also involved in the root meaning of the Latin word. *Religo* means to tie up, or bind. People who don't want to be tied up in any way don't want religion. But we can't have a social order without some restraints. We need laws and lawmakers and administrators. And if there is no law recognized above the lawmakers and administrators they tend to become tyrants. Even if the will of the people is recognized as above that of the rulers this will tends to become tyrannical, or splits into selfish class interests and resultant chaos, unless it recognizes a higher will above it that is concerned with the good of all. This is the lesson of history.

If a people to any great extent loses its religion it relapses into chaos or slavery. We see this in ancient Greece and modern Germany and among many primitive tribes. Anthropologists constantly warn administrators who have to deal with primitive people that they must respect tribal religion, change it only gradually, always waiting until some equally effective belief can take the place of the old, or they will demoralize the tribe. There was a great loss of religion in ancient Greece which was followed by chaos and tyranny. Newly won liberties of the democracies were lost to dictatorships because they recognized no adequate restraints. Enlightened and democratic Athens made herself an imperialistic tyrant and brought resultant ruin upon herself. The old Greek religion, which had given some cohesion to the early Greek tribes and social order, was inadequate and out of date by the time of Pericles. Some of the Greek philosophers tried to purify it and improve it. But their influence was too little and too late. Greek society could find no higher law, in which men sufficiently believed, to keep within bounds the selfishness of individuals, classes and petty states. Division, violence and injustice went unchecked, and at last the quarreling communities fell under the tyranny first of Macedon and then of Rome. Some degree of order was restored, but liberty was lost.

Loss of religion is not the only cause of social chaos, reaction and decay. But it is significant that where religion loses its influence, either through unbelief or by failing to keep up with the life of the times, social disaster tends to follow. The French Revolution is an example of this tendency. The controlling hierarchy of the church had become so corrupt and so closely connected with the effete and predatory ruling class that it became the opponent of necessary reform. The democratic regime sought clumsily to reform the church, with resultant clash of consciences and moral confusion. The Paris mob fell under the influence of antireligious leaders, who led it to terrible extremes. The terror and moral confusion thus initiated made impossible the difficult task of welding the contending parties into a stable democracy, and from chaos the republic passed into the dictatorship of Napoleon.

France still suffers from lack of a religion that can retain the respect of independent thinkers and support popular reforms. Atheism is today very widespread among the upper classes. And atheism recognizes no moral law above purely human desires. It can find no logical reason why any individual or class should sacrifice its own interests for those of another. So when many of these people became convinced that it was in their individual interest and that of their class to collaborate with Hitler rather than fight for democracy they did so. Except for a sense of shame and love of France many others would have done so.   The forces of resistance have been found, in France as in the rest of Europe, chiefly in two places.   First, among those who, like General de Gaulle, believed in liberty and human rights on religious grounds.   Even Pétain was saved by his religion from complete cooperation with the Nazis.   Second, among the Communists who, though they do not believe in God as source of a higher moral law, nevertheless have a deep personal interest in and a strong loyalty to another type of social order (opposed to fascism) which they believe is destined to triumph.

Because of its very definite philosophy and political program, communism has almost the effect of religion in giving drive and direction to ethical ideals.   But it has a narrow class outlook on present-day problems and encourages ruthlessness in dealing with them.   Stalin's harsh treatment of kulaks and Trotzkyists is quite consistent with Marxian ethics.   But the Russian people as a whole have not lost their religion.   And the Russian church has for many years given support to the Soviet economic program.   It has also helped buttress the spiritual resistance of the people in the trials of war.   Stalin has shown his wisdom in that, though himself still an unbeliever, he has come to recognize the value of religion in the life of the state.

RELIGION IN CHINA

Another example of social collapse following on loss of religious support is to be found in modern China. The Chinese have not lost their religion, but they have lost the connection between their political system and their ancient religion.   Confucianism, like every other historic religion, is a mixture of truth and error.   It contains many noble teachings, but it is not adapted to modern conditions. It teaches that there is a supreme being, identified with Heaven, who is the source of the moral law. The principal duty of this moral law is filial piety, honor and obedience to one's parents. The whole empire is one great family, with the emperor as its rightful head. The emperor is the son of Heaven. He alone worships Heaven on behalf of his people, who pay reverence to their own ancestors and may worship minor deities, but not Heaven. Thus the emperor is the sole link between Heaven and the common man, and his authority is unquestionable so long as he wields it in accord with the laws of Heaven — laws which even the common man finds imprinted in his heart, and which teach him benevolence, justice, wisdom, sincerity and propriety.

This noble religion was well adapted to the needs of the Chinese people until modern times. It supported an orderly civilized life, peace, and classical culture over the vast area of China. But the Manchu Dynasty stood in the way of progress. The young Chinese who had been educated abroad saw the intellectual flaws in the system. In 1911 they conspired to overthrow the imperial dynasty and established in its place a democratic republic.

But for the common people this took the keystone out of the arch of their moral and political system. The new president was not the son of Heaven, and did not claim to be. There was no higher divine law supporting his authority, or that of the officials appointed by him, or that of the elected members of the new legislative bodies. Ambitious men swiftly began to turn their new power to their own interests. Civil war, corruption and banditry spread throughout the land. At length a little company of sincere patriots, led by a Christian medical man, Sun Yat Sen, and Chiang Kai-shek, gained control of the city of Canton, and set out to unify the country.

The inspiration of this movement lay in the conviction of its leaders that the divine law upholds, not the authority of an emperor, but the right of the people to life and security, to the means of livelihood and the opportunity for self-government. They stated their ideal in terms drawn from China's ancient ethics. Patriotism and the bitter lessons of chaos have combined to win acceptance for it. It has become to millions of Chinese a new religion, whether or not directly associated with the Christianity which is its source. It is this combination of patriotism, ethics and religion, underlying the new democratic movement in China, that gives it hope for success where the earlier movement failed.

RELIGION IN EUROPE

Turning again to Europe we find the prime example of social collapse following loss of religion in Nazi Germany. Nowhere in the world has the modern spread of unbelief gone further than in Germany. But it has gone far among all the other peoples of Europe too. Germany is merely the extreme case of a general symptom. And much of the blame for this state of affairs must be laid on the religious organizations of Europe.

In the English-speaking world, tolerance — the right to freedom of thought and speech on religious matters — was asserted and acknowledged as a *religious* principle back in the days when religious issues were still the most vital and serious questions before the minds of men. In Europe religious freedom was not granted until people had begun to grow indifferent to religious questions.

The state churches attempted to suppress all noncon-
formity, and largely succeeded. To do this they allied
themselves in every way with the powers dominant in the
state. Thus, in Europe, any opposition to the existing
class rule had perforce to oppose the church. The liberal and democratic movement therefore became an antireligious movement. In England and America, on the
contrary, it found its inspiration and support in those
churches that had broken with the state church in the
name of freedom of conscience.

This situation reveals one of the points where the religious man needs to exercise eternal vigilance and frequently fails. The central thought of religion is that of
a divine moral law which is above the desires of men.
Thus religion becomes a great buttress of the social order
that society has developed for its own welfare and believes to be good. It is easy then to identify the existing
law of the land with the divine will, instead of recognizing that, at its best, it is but a fallible human attempt to
execute the divine will. A lazy habit of mind tends to
grow to regard the constitution as sacred, whether it is
monarchical, aristocratic or democratic. And this is all
the easier for those who benefit by special privileges under the constitution. Churches and churchmen that are
given special privileges are not the least guilty in this
respect.

Thus there arose in Europe an alliance between privi-
leged classes in church and state. Those who were injured by these special privileges naturally came to regard
the church as their enemy, as well as the ruling class in
the state. There was no other religious group in the
community, recognized, tolerated and strong, from
whom they could receive inspiration and help. So they

became antireligious, rebelling against the existing economic and political order, and hating and despising the religious organization that supported injustice in the name of God. In England and America these same tendencies are present, but to a lesser degree. Liberal and democratic movements have found leaders in free and democratic churches; in England, recently, also in the state church. Communism is a foreign rather than a native movement in both countries.

On the European continent, however, the battle lines were tightly drawn. The Greek and Roman Catholic churches and the Protestant state churches, with only minor exceptions, have tended to support political reaction. Political radicalism has been antireligious. As a result the church has lost in spiritual power, has failed in its social function, which is to be the most sensitive part of the community conscience, calling attention to evil and injustice on every hand. It has also lost the confidence of the masses of the community whom it ought to have aided in their struggle. And it has lost the respect of the upper classes themselves, because it has condoned their selfishness when it should have condemned it. Further, because it had lost respect and was failing in its function, it failed to attract into its leadership that great supply of able and sincere men which it needs. It became intellectually sluggish, conservative and backward. Or else it slavishly gave way to the vigorous attacks of intellectuals and watered down its teaching to something meaningless, instead of thinking its way boldly through the problems created by modern science and history.

This indictment of the church in Europe may sound too strong. And it could be turned, though with less-

ened force, against the churches of the English-speaking
world. But it remains true that in Europe, to a greater
degree than in Britain and America, and in Germany to
the greatest degree of all, the Christian churches before
the war had lost the respect of both the upper and lower
classes of the community. Religion was at a low ebb.

Just at this time Europe, and especially Germany, were
required to face a double crisis which called for high
moral resolution and idealism. One feature of this crisis
was the rise of nationalism. Throughout the nineteenth
century the peoples of Europe had been steadily winning
their independence and unity. National pride everywhere aspired to gather all those of one distinctive speech
and culture into a distinctive national unit and make it
great. This process culminated in the treaty of Ver-
sailles. It was impossible to satisfy the conflicting aspirations of all countries and many of the decisions naturally went against defeated Germany. It was a hard blow
for this strong and proud people to see other nations'
aspirations satisfied, but not theirs; some even at their
expense. National pride called for justice — and revenge. The other feature of the crisis was the economic
blizzard that swept across the world from 1929 to 1935.
It called for high statesmanship to adjust the claims of
contending classes, all of whom felt injured by a course
of events beyond their control.

Difficult times always tempt us to seek remedies that
lie outside the moral law. Germany, having lost too
much of that religion which supports the moral law, lis-
tened to the tempter. " It is not your fault that you are
beaten in battle and poor. It is the Jews. They be-
trayed you; and they filch your money and your jobs
from you. Revenge yourselves on them. Turn them

out of their jobs. Take their money. Run them out of
the country. Build yourselves an army again. The
chance will come to use it. You are the superior race.
You can impose your will on others. You can avenge
their insults. You can make yourselves rich on the
spoils." It was a seductive program. Martin Luther or
Immanuel Kant would have scorned it. They believed
in an eternal moral law. But too many of the Germans
of the twentieth century had ceased to believe in any law
above national self-interest. They made the tempter
their leader and gave him the power he asked for to carry
out his plan. They made themselves his slaves and he
led them to disaster.

In all the dark picture there has been just one bright
spot. The German church rose up from its slumber
and insignificance to become almost the sole source of
resistance to the evil program of the dictator. The intellectuals (for the most part) and the universities suc-
cumbed and took their orders. The newspapers, the
trade unions and the leaders of commerce fell into line
and goose-stepped. But in the churches there was a considerable section who at length opened their eyes to see
the evil program for what it was. It was too late to stop
it. But it was not too late to protest, to resist, and to
suffer. By their heroism these religious leaders of Germany, whatever their earlier faults, have earned title to
respect. They indicate that the great tragedy of the
twentieth century could not have happened had not Germany so largely lost her religion.

RELIGION IN THE POSTWAR WORLD

These historical facts show plainly that man has not
outgrown the *need* of religion. Religion is still needed to

support the moral law which underlies the social structure and to provide a court of appeal from evils that appear in the legalized social structure to a higher law which
is concerned equally with the good of all. *The lesson of
history is that where religion is weak any crisis in a nation's history that puts a strain on the moral resources of
its people is apt to end in moral breakdown and social
chaos;* and chaos ends in loss of freedom, in foreign con-
quest or local dictatorship.

One does not need to be a prophet to foresee that
America and all the other democracies will, in the near
future, be faced by problems in which the moral conscience of the people will need all the support it can de-
rive from religion. We have to guide the destinies of a
new world organization without either developing a new
imperialism or relapsing into isolationism. The British
commonwealth must liquidate its imperialism. America
must solve its race problem. The problem of mass un-
employment has only been postponed by war; the solution has yet to be found. In our economy, wealth still
tends to accumulate too much in the hands of the few
while millions are " ill-fed, ill-housed, and ill-clothed."

These problems will try our souls. They call for
wisdom guided by a strong national sense of justice, obligation, good will and respect for personality. The self-
interest of individuals and of great economic and political pressure groups must be restrained. Can it be done
if we lose the sense of a higher law above the individual's
desire for his own success and happiness? Can it be done
without an adequate religion?

Leaders of social movements for the improvement of
the lot of the depressed classes have not sufficiently realized the importance of the moral element in politics.

They have put their trust in group self-interest and the power of the majority vote or the threat of mass revolution. They have not awakened to the fact that in a modern industrial society the depressed classes are no longer a majority. No more than one-third of our American people are " ill-fed, ill-housed and ill-clothed." It is the majority who profit from the cheap labor and bad conditions imposed on the minority. If each group votes only according to its self-interest that majority will continue to maintain this situation.

The middle class holds the balance of voting power and, from the purely economic standpoint, it is not in its interest to unite with the poor to rectify their injustices at the expense of the rich. If the injustices of the poor are to be rectified it must be done by appeal to the sense of justice of the middle class to vote for reform, even at some cost to themselves. If this is to be done we shall need all the support of religion in the appeal to the middle-class sense of justice. And we shall need the leadership of those whose political activities are inspired by religious ideals.

Communists, in attacking religion, are undermining their best source of support in their efforts on behalf of the dispossessed. Because the religious institutions of nineteenth-century Europe supported the traditional aristocratic and capitalistic conceptions of the state the Marxians attacked religion. And because of their materialistic philosophy they did not believe in the power of moral motives to institute reforms. So they concluded that the situation could not be remedied without force. They worked for the revolution. And they were met by the counterrevolution of fascism. They are now a hundred years behind the times. Revolution by force can no longer remedy the wrongs of the poor, for the rich are possessed of all the powerful weapons and have the support of the great middle class. The " increasing misery of the proletariat " is a myth; and so is the theory of its increasing numbers. The day of popular revolutions is over for modern nations. Only fascist revolutions are now possible. The only hope for the common man lies in democracy. And the only hope *there* lies in a national sense of justice backed by religion.

ETHICS WITHOUT RELIGION

Those who contend that we ought to have outgrown religion usually support their position by saying that enlightened self-interest is enough if only it is sufficiently enlightened. There is no need, they argue, of any higher law to require of a man that he should be just, generous, courageous and honest in his dealings with his fellows. It is in his true interest to be so. Such conduct maintains an orderly society in which he can live securely and happily. It wins him that respect and friendship without which few can be successful and none happy. Above all, it maintains his own inner self-respect, which is vitally important, for no external pleasures and successes can compensate for the inner dissatisfaction a man feels if he is contemptible in his own esteem.

In answer to this we should point out that, so long as a man considers only his external worldly interests, apart from the inner demands of his own self-respect, it is often to his interest (in this narrow sense) to ignore the rights and welfare of others, especially when the great majority of his own associates, his own class or community, do the same. The easy way is always to go with the crowd. In a community of cheats honesty is not always the best policy. Further, if bad social situations are to be remedied someone must protest and take the consequences of scorn and hatred. The prophets of social justice are likely to be stoned. And martyrs are not produced by motives of external and worldly self-interest, however enlightened.

But what of the final argument for the ethics of self-interest — the need to maintain one's spiritual integrity, one's inner self-respect? The answer here is, first, that most people respect the sort of person they have been taught to respect. Their conscience does not rise above the common level. They therefore tolerate in themselves whatever actions they find generally condoned by those around them. " Others do it," they say, " so why shouldn't I?" The demands of conscience, or inner self-respect, will never raise a person above the common level around him unless he does a great deal of serious and self-critical thinking on moral issues. But few do this. And why should they if the result is only to develop a sensitive conscience that will stand in the way of their other desires? So most people are content to be as good, morally, as the next person. And it is easy for a man to persuade himself that he is as good as the next person when really he is not. Thus the moral standard tends gradually to fall instead of rise — unless people believe that it is fixed by an authority higher than their own self-interest and the opinions of those round about them.

Against this the objection is still urged that there are, in fact, many people who do not believe in God, but who nevertheless maintain fine characters and make many personal sacrifices for the common good. This is, of course, true. It may even be the case that, in a community where there is a general belief in God, the character of the few unbelievers is above that of the general level of the believers. The unbeliever must be a person of intelligence and mental vigor to think his way to a view so vitally different from that of the great majority. Such a person readily absorbs the best in the moral tradition, with critical discrimination as to its real meaning. He desires the respect of the community and cultivates the virtues which win that respect. He feels keenly the inner need to maintain his own personal integrity and so is loyal to the truth as he sees it when the evidence seems to him to be against the commonly accepted religious beliefs. He may even sacrifice external, worldly interests for the inner satisfaction of maintaining the integrity and freedom of his own thought. He is to be honored for doing so. One of the great mistakes of religious people has been the persecution of such men. The term " atheist " should never be used with scorn or contempt. Most of those in our community to whom it is applicable are persons of good character and honest seekers of truth.

But the atheist's character is maintained by his conscience, supported by his inner self-respect. It would make him unhappy to do things that he has learned to regard as contemptible. But why does he regard it as contemptible to commit an injustice even when it is in his external and worldly interests to do so? Why does he regard it as fine and admirable to be just and generous, honest and courageous even to the point of personal self-sacrifice? It is because these ideals are the essential part of the moral tradition in which he has been trained — a tradition developed and preserved by the religion in which the general community believes. Why do the Nazi storm troopers not regard it as contemptible to kick a harmless Jew in the stomach? It is because the great group of Germans to which they belong has lost its belief in the authority of the Christian moral tradition and replaced it by a creed of race superiority and brute force. Why have nominally Christian mobs sometimes done the same sort of thing? Because they have not thoroughly absorbed the finer part of the Christian tradition so as to incorporate it into their proper self-respect, or because they have allowed their temporary passion to drive them to do things of which they are subsequently ashamed.

There can be no doubt that these ideals of justice, generosity, courage and honesty have been developed and maintained by religion. Among primitive men religion supports the tribal moral code, which asserts that every tribesman has duties to his fellows, whether they are in accord with his own interests or not. Gradually this code is extended — to the visiting stranger, to friendly tribes, to all mankind, even to enemies. Tribal religions have supported the narrower moralities, but the prophets of religious progress have initiated and supported the expansion of the concept of duty against individual and group self-interest. They have based this obligation on the conception of a God who is source and support of the moral law and have argued that because God takes an interest in the welfare of other persons and other peoples so too should we.

It is difficult to see in what other way this broad universal conception of man's moral obligations can be logically maintained. Whether it can we shall inquire in our next chapter. For the present we simply note that historically it was religion that developed the concept of universal obligation and that religion still sustains it. Any other basis, even if one can be found, must for long be socially weak and precarious.

The study of ethics without religion leads then to these conclusions: (*a*) that a pursuit of one's external and worldly self-interest alone does not produce the kind of character society needs; (*b*) that the further development of character depends on a person's inner self-respect, demanding of him that he live up to an ideal set by his conscience; (*c*) that the ideals his conscience upholds are first shaped by the moral tradition he is taught in his youth and can be modified only by critical thinking; (*d*) that, historically, it is the critical thinking of religious teachers that has shaped our moral tradition and developed our ideals of universal justice and good will; (*e*) that when the religious standard is rejected people are easily diverted to standards set up by special groups in their own special interests, e.g., those of race, nation and class.

THE INTELLECTUAL PROBLEM

From the practical standpoint, then, it is evident that we have not outgrown the *need* of religion. But the question still presses: Is there any proof of the truth of religion? Are there any rational grounds for believing in a divine authority for the moral law? And how can we know what is the moral law to which it bears witness? Religions differ in their moral codes. And some of their doctrines are plainly false and superstitious. On others they contradict each other. Those who say we ought to have outgrown religion are usually thinking of the inadequacies and errors of our present religion — the conservative and often reactionary political tendencies of some religious institutions, the outworn creeds that have lost the respect of the majority of intelligent and edu-

cated persons, the occasional opposition to freedom of
thought and scientific teaching, the rigid and narrow
moral principles insisted upon by some churches.

These faults of contemporary religion are to be de-
plored. It is part of the purpose of this book to expose
them and show how unnecessary they are to a strong and
true religion. But even a poor religion is, in the long
run, usually better than none. So long as a religion
maintains the essential conviction that a man's obligations to his fellows are rooted in a higher law than the
mere pursuit of his own earthly happiness it performs its
essential function. It is possible for the religion to be so
full of injurious superstitions as to outweigh the value of
its central truth. But this is not often so. In any case,
the remedy is not to abolish the religion, but to purify
and improve it.

So we must pass now to our main theme — an inquiry
into the truth of religion. Society needs religion. But
it needs a better religion than it has had in the past. And
it needs more assurance than it has had of the truth of
its religious ideas. We need God. But where can we
find him? How can we know his will? Why does he not
reveal himself?

The answer, in brief, is that God is ever with us, that
he reveals himself to us constantly so far as we need to
know him and in the only way in which we could pos-
sibly be assured and understand. But we are very slow
to recognize him for what he is. The finite children of
God must grow gradually in the knowledge of their Father. For if they were not finite they would be God.
And if they did not have to grow they would be not children, but mere things.

Where Do We Find God?

GOD AS SOURCE OF THE MORAL LAW

WHEN WE are faced with a question such as this chapter sets before us it is a good rule of logic first to define our terms. What do we mean by " God "? But right here it is possible to make a serious mistake. In the course of centuries Jews and Christians have come to adopt a very elaborate conception of God as an eternal Being, infinite in goodness and wisdom, omnipotent, omnipresent, creator of all things, giver of the moral law. But this is quite a lot to set out to prove! It is easy for the critic to pick on to some of these conceptions and to point out their difficulties. How can we reconcile God's alleged goodness and omnipotence with the existence of terrible evils like tornadoes and earthquakes, disease and insanity? Why do we need to believe in a creator when evolution explains the development of all the different forms of life? How can we know that any being is infinite or eternal? Faced with these problems the theologian has to delve deep into metaphysics and science. His arguments grow too intricate to be clear and convincing. The ordinary person is lost.

Let us begin with a much simpler conception that contains at least what is most essential. We have already seen that man tends to believe in God, not out of wishful thinking, desiring to believe in a powerful helper in his troubles, but because he feels that the authority of the

23

moral law rests in something greater than himself or any priest or king or other human authority. The god of man's early religious beliefs is first and foremost the sustainer of the moral law, whatever else he may be. We also saw that the important function religion performs for society is, first, to uphold the fundamental moral law on which the social structure rests and, second, to offer authority for a higher moral law in the light of which the prophets and reformers can criticize the existing law of the land when it works badly. So let us begin with this simpler conception. Our question then will mean: Can we find any authority for the moral law higher than that of man? This will also involve the question: Can we know what the moral law really is? When we search for the origin of the moral law we shall discover that there is something within ourselves which demands of us that we concern ourselves disinterestedly with the good of others. And further inquiry will disclose that this " something " is God.

THE ETHICS OF SELF-INTEREST AND LOYALTY

In discussing the question whether self-interest is an adequate guide for the moral life we took notice of the assertion, made by critics of religion, that a man's own inner self-respect demands of him that he be just, generous and honest in his dealings with his fellows. We replied that this moral self-respect, or conscience, which demands of him that he consider the interests of others besides himself and which makes him feel contemptible if he does not, has been developed and shaped by a religious tradition. This raised the question whether conscience can be maintained at this high level without the influence of religion in the community.

It has already been pointed out that such an ideal cannot be based on self-interest at the level of external and worldly interests. One person's worldly interests clash with another's. The private interests of individuals and groups are not always consistent with the general public interest. If we argue, " You must be just to others or you cannot expect them to be just to you," the answer comes too easily, " I don't believe they will always be just to me, so I can't afford to be always just to them." If any man is ashamed to give such an answer it must be because he believes in an ideal of conduct that is above self-interest. In brief, the moral ideal requires that an individual should sometimes sacrifice his own interests for the good of the community, and it is logically impossible to base an appeal for self-sacrifice on self-interest.

In practice such appeals are commonly based, not on self-interest, but on a motive that is often much more powerful and always much more admired — that of loyalty to the group, to friends or family, comrades or country. Man is a social animal and deep-rooted social tendencies attach him to the social groups to which he belongs. Every normal person is ashamed not to be loyal. Here, certainly, is one of the reasons why a certain concern for the good of others forms part of the ideal of conduct demanded of us by our inner self-respect.

But loyalties are always narrow. They not only *attach* us to groups; they also *divide* us into groups. They hold us to one group and set us against others. If there is a loyalty toward the human race as a whole it is inevitably weak beside the loyalties to the narrower groups which enter so much more directly and deeply into our lives. So if it were simply our loyalties that produced in us the moral ideal, that ideal would never carry us beyond fam-

ily and tribal morality. But this is merely the sort of
morality that people tend to revert to when they lose
their religion. They become, at best, good friends, good
comrades, good Americans — or good Nazis. At this
level people feel it contemptible to injure or betray the
group. But they must rise to a higher level if they are to
feel that it is contemptible, for some relatively small
benefit to themselves or their own group, to injure or
betray an outsider.

THE WILL TO THE GREATEST GOOD

Neither self-interest nor loyalty, then, can form an
adequate basis for an ethic that asserts the universal and
equal rights of all. Yet such an ethic has won almost universal approval in the Golden Rule taught by both Christ
and Confucius and in such principles as the utilitarian
slogan of " the greatest happiness of the greatest number." On what can this approval be based? Is there, in
human nature itself, some *general* principle of good will
to all mankind? If so, is it strong enough to account for
the fact that these high ethical ideals have come to be
almost everywhere endorsed, even though, in practice,
we fall far short of them?

Reflection on this question shows that there is such a
principle. There is something within us which *demands
of us that we concern ourselves disinterestedly with the
good of others besides ourselves.* It makes itself felt
when we reflect, when we sit down in a cool hour and
think about the pleasures and pains, joys and sorrows, of
other human beings — or indeed of any living creatures.
It also responds impulsively when we see another's pleasure or pain. We tend *naturally* to be glad that others are
glad and sad that others are sad. This tendency is a part

of human nature. It is so distinctive of human nature that we say of those who manifest it strongly that they are " humane." We remark of such a person that " he is very human." We call the opposite qualities " inhuman."

We may call this " the general tendency to seek the good," because it is not specially concerned with the good of any particular person, either one's self or friend. Nor is it specially concerned with any particular kind of good. It is just that whatever appeals to us as good is something that we naturally wish should exist, apart from any question as to whose good it is or what may be its further consequences. Because it has no special interest or bias we say it is " disinterested."

When we go on to pay attention to distinctions of *whose* good, or further consequences, this, of course, may change our wish. The small good that brings very bad consequences we view as evil " as a whole "; we then wish that, as a whole, it should not exist; and we tend to act accordingly. The question of whose good may also affect our action. We form special habits of desiring the good of some people, especially our own self, more strongly than that of others. This habit may make the wish for the *lesser* good of self or friend stronger than the wish for the *greater* good of some other person, where the wish for the good has not been strengthened by the growth of habit. This choice of the lesser good we often call " evil." But it is not really a wish to produce evil. It is merely that the wish for a certain good has acquired extra strength through habit and thus overrides the wish for the other good.

This strength of habit often leads to choice of the lesser good even for one's self. We may reflectively recognize a certain good as the greater; but when the moment for action comes old habits assert themselves and we reach for the good that is near and familiar. Again, this choice of the lesser good we may reflectively call " evil." But it was not due to a wish for evil — for sorrow, pain or disappointment. It was due to a habit-strengthened wish for a certain minor good. Animal appetites and natural emotional tendencies or " instincts " may similarly upset our more deliberate choices of the greater good.

What looks much more like an actual wish to produce evil for its own sake occurs in anger. But anger is a secondary reaction. We have wished for certain goods and found our efforts to produce them interfered with. This arouses a wish to do something to the source of interference so that it can no longer interfere; and this wish is commonly reinforced by the emotional feeling we call anger. Emotion makes us blind; it concentrates attention on a single wish so that we don't think of other consequences. If the infliction of pain, or even death, upon the person interfering with our other wishes appears as the means to prevent his interference, then we tend to wish that pain or death upon him. And if emotion sufficiently blinds us to the consequences we may try to carry it out. If a person very frequently interferes with our desires we may so get the habit of wishing pain or destruction to prevent him that we begin to think of any evil to him as a good to ourselves. This is the attitude we call hatred. But it is still true that anger and hatred are secondary reactions. The wishing of evil upon the other person is due to a tendency first established as a means to a certain further good for the self or friends or friendly group. It may be a wish for a lesser good, but it is one that is reinforced by habit or natural emotional impulses.

THE SENSE OF RIGHT AND WRONG

In all these cases, therefore, we see that the human wish is a wish for a good. And normally, of course, we wish for the greatest possible good. But acquired habits, animal appetites, and instinctive, emotional impulses reinforce certain wishes and often lead us to pursue the lesser good. For the most part these habits and other impulses lead us to choose our own private good. And when they do so at the cost of the greater good of others we call this "selfishness" and say it is wrong.

Now here is a very familiar fact that is truly remarkable. But it is so familiar we do not realize how remarkable it is. It is really extraordinary that we should ever think it wrong to do anything so natural as to pursue our strongest wishes. But we do. If ever we sit down and coolly consider the fact that we chose the lesser of two possible goods we feel that there was something wrong about that choice. It is the same if we have chosen a good at the cost of an evil that outweighs it. This would be easily intelligible if we felt this way only when the greater good lost, or the greater evil incurred, is our own. But we tend to feel that it is wrong also to pursue our own lesser good at the cost of losing some greater good (or incurring some greater evil) for another person.

We feel this most strongly when it is the good of some friend or member of our own social group that we have thus neglected for our own lesser good. There are two reasons for this, both rooted in habit. In the first place we have learned (or acquired the habit) from the community to think of such actions as wrong. Second, the wish to produce the good of friends and neighbors is always reinforced by habit, so that the conflicting nature of our action is more strongly impressed upon us.

But we cannot explain the whole sense of wrong as due to the teaching of the community. For if the community (e.g., a Nazi community) should say that to seek a benefit for one's self at the cost of a definitely greater injury to another person is all right in certain special cases (e.g., if the other person is a Jew), then it is possible for a member of that (Nazi) community to see that in this case *his community is wrong*. And he *will* see this if only he will think hard enough and without special prejudice.

In the early stages of moral development each social group tended to confine its sense of obligation to its own members, because their own habits and the comments of those around them drew their attention to wrongs done to their own people, but not to others. Also, emotional prejudices, springing from fear and anger, tended to blind them in the case of wrongs done to members of another group. But some individuals did some hard and unprejudiced thinking on these questions and came to feel that it is also wrong, for the sake of some relatively small personal benefit, to bring injury on a stranger. When these thinkers first expressed this view they were met with opposition and derision, for people do not like to have their habits interfered with or to have obligations thrust upon them. But the thinkers persisted and made other people think. And when the others *thought* enough about it they began to feel the same way. So eventually the stranger was accorded his rights. And gradually man came to recognize that what is *really* right is always to do the best for all concerned.

It was a lesson human beings did not learn willingly, for it is so much against man's habits and impulses which tend to pursue our own good first. Even when people came to recognize the principle as right they still failed to live up to it, and made all sorts of excuses for exceptions to the rule. For habits and traditions are very strong. But almost everywhere now it is recognized by those who think, and think without prejudice, on questions of right and wrong, that we ought to do in every case what seems best for all concerned.

This result has come about by thoughtful analysis of our sense of right and wrong, as we feel it. And thoughtful analysis could not have produced this general conclusion if it were not that there is *something in our nature which demands of us that we seek the good of others equally with our own*. It is not merely that we wish for the good of the other person. We do that, but usually we wish more strongly for our own. It is not merely that we wish for the greatest good. We do that, too; but we also often wish more strongly for some lesser good — for ourselves or our own group. It is rather that there is an " ought," a " sense of obligation," attached to the idea of the greatest good. The will to realize it has a unique sort of authority. If, by force of habit or impulse, we override it for the sake of some lesser good, it has the power of impressing upon us, in subsequent reflection, that we did wrong. We can refuse to reflect and blindly follow habit, tradition and personal preference. We can shake off the sense of wrong by ceasing to reflect. But we cannot *think* about questions of good and evil, right and wrong, without finding that the will to the greatest good

of all concerned tends to break through our selfishness
and the limitations established by group tradition. It
breaks through and asserts its authority. All that conflicts with it is wrong.

THE WILL THAT IS FIRST AND LAST

Our analysis has shown that this sense of an " ought "
is attached to the will to the greatest good. This will,
with its " ought," is a part of the self. It may not be as
strong as the wishes that have acquired the force of habit
or are backed by native impulse and emotion; but in reflective thought it asserts its peculiar authority. Whatever impulse or desire is out of harmony with it, it brands
as " wrong." To be wrong is to miss the goal at which
one aims, or to be out of harmony with an acknowledged
standard. So the choice of the lesser good is said to be
out of harmony with some standard or to miss its real
aim, even if it obtains that lesser good. The will to the
greatest good asserts itself as right. And it asserts that
the *real* aim of the self in every act of will is also the
greatest good, but that in pursuing this lesser good
(through force of habit or natural impulse) it is off its
course, missing its mark. The assertion is that the real
aim, the fundamental purpose, of every self is to produce
the greatest good, whether that be for itself or for some
other.

This means that any pursuit of any particular good is
simply a part of a larger aim, a means to an end. The ultimate end is always the greatest possible good. But this
ultimate end is commonly forgotten in attention to the
means. The means is itself a good; and having found it
good one may pursue it for its own sake and in ways that
defeat the end. Thus, for example, a man desires health.

For his health he decides to take exercise. He finds the exercise good and takes too much, impairing his health. From the standpoint of health he has done wrong; he has missed the mark. Similarly, the *sufficiently reflective* moral conscience asserts that our ultimate goal is to produce the greatest possible good. We find that possession of money is a means to much good. We enjoy and take pride in possession of it and pursue the possession of money at the cost of some greater good to some other person. In reflection we discover that this is wrong. It has missed the mark, the true end, the ultimate goal.

Now the will to the end is not merely the last act of will in the series of efforts that work toward a goal. It is also the first. And it remains as the set, directing purpose, in the background of consciousness, all the way through. So the assertion that our ultimate goal is the production of the greatest possible good means that the will to the greatest good is not merely the final form, the highest development, of the moral life; it is also its fundamental beginning.

This means that in the simplest beginning of human consciousness, will takes the form of an effort to produce good, more good, always greater and greater good. In this effort it forms specific habits which in general serve its purpose and add to its power to pursue further good. It acquires knowledge of many different kinds of good and different means to good. It cannot keep all these in mind at once, nor can it keep its ultimate goal ever clearly before it. But in each situation it responds to what it feels or anticipates as good, seeking to maintain and expand it. Gradually it develops the capacity of analyzing a situation and distinguishing alternative possibilities of action. More or less accurately it foresees the

end of each action and makes its choice according to
which promises the greater good. Thus it modifies its
habits and develops new ones.

For the first few years of a human life there is no
awareness of any goods other than its own immediate
sensory pleasures and natural satisfactions. These are
the goods it pursues; and it forms a strong set of habits
of pursuing such goods without much analysis of alternative possibilities. But gradually the child becomes
aware of other selves as also having pleasures and pains,
satisfactions and dissatisfactions. When the child becomes aware of these he spontaneously seeks to produce
these goods too — goods he does not himself feel. As
soon as a mother can make the child understand that
she too enjoys eating candy the child will manifest a desire to put candy into her mouth, and will show much
pleasure in doing what he has come to understand brings
pleasure to the other person. This means that as soon
as the child learns that he *can* create pleasure in another
person's experience he spontaneously *wants* to do so. He
is not indirectly seeking his own pleasure. He gets pleasure out of doing it only because he *first* has the desire to
do it — to create a good he does not himself immediately
experience. Gradually he then forms habits of pursuing
this other sort of good besides his own.

But now arise new possibilities of conflicts between
his desires. He desires the good of other people and of
himself. He has a well established set of habits of seeking his own goods, i.e., his own pleasures and satisfactions. These often conflict with what he sees to be the
greater good of other persons. At first, habit is usually
dominant. But occasionally he reflects on such choices
and then he begins to feel something vaguely wrong

about them. The impulse to pursue his own good was stronger at the time of action because it was reinforced by habit. It was the familiar, easy and assured line of action. But in reflection the good obtained appears definitely smaller compared to the good lost or the evil produced — for the other person. The choice of the lesser good appears somehow to have missed his real aim.

At length he realizes that he now wishes, and has always wished, to produce the greater good. In similar instances in the past, when he has neglected or destroyed the greater good, or produced an evil overbalancing the good, he has been told such acts are "naughty" or "wrong." He now has a new experience to attach to that word. It has acquired new meaning. On a subsequent occasion he remembers how such actions appeared in later reflection. He controls the habitual impulse and pursues the greater good. Gradually such choices become habitual and easy. He has become socially adapted. He has formed a good character. He has become a well integrated personality because he has brought his major habits into harmony with that will to the greatest good which is first and last, the beginning and the end of his volitional life.

MORAL EFFORT AND PERSONAL INTEGRITY

We can see now where all those attempts to trace moral conduct to enlightened self-interest are wrong. They interpret human will as originally and essentially an effort to obtain something seen as " good-for-me." In reality, *will is originally and essentially neutral as between the self in which it occurs and other selves.* It is simply a response to the quality of value that enters into the life of feeling. It prefers pleasure to pain, beauty to ugliness, joy to sorrow. We lump all these together when we say it prefers good to evil. It seeks ever the greatest good within the horizon of its feeling and thought.

At first the only goods within that horizon are those of its own self, as immediately felt. At this stage the will never hesitates. It goes for the greatest, the one that is most strongly felt. It avoids the felt evils or pains. Later the individual develops the capacity to anticipate future goods; and now some hesitation arises. It has formed the habit of paying attention to what is present. When the future good appears greater than the present some effort is required to break through this habit and pay attention to the more distant goal. But it learns to do this and directs its behavior accordingly. At length the individual develops the capacity to recognize the existence of other selves and imaginatively to enter into their experience and see that they too have pleasures and pains, joys and sorrows. Here is a new cause of hesitation. The habit of paying attention to the self's own goods conflicts with the tendency to pursue the greatest good when that is the good of some other self. It requires some effort of will to break through the habit, pay attention to the good of others, and act accordingly. But when the will makes that effort it is true to its own essential nature. When it fails it is the slave of habit.

Now we must not make the mistake of setting up a complete distinction between habit and will. A habitual action can, in some circumstances, be carried out automatically and unconsciously. In so far as this is the case the action is not willed. It is involuntary. But so long as we are aware of our goal and of what we are doing our actions are willed (i.e., voluntary), however familiar and habitual. Every wish or want is an act of will, even the wishes or wants of our natural appetites. A conflict between two desires is a conflict of will. Will is not an indivisible unit, except in its simplest possible form where there is no awareness of alternatives. So every habit is simply a specialized form of will, become familiar, easy, strong and ready through frequent practice. A habit is the development of a capacity to perform certain voluntary actions with ease and power and with little attention. The growth of habits adds to our capacity to perform complex actions and to deal with complex situations with accuracy and assurance. It frees attention to look further afield and analyze the unfamiliar.

It is now a generally recognized conception of modern psychology that an individual personality is simply an organized bundle of habits. An individual mind is a more or less well integrated set of habitual tendencies to attend to this, that and the other thing — a set of habits of thought and action. But each habitual act, as we have seen, is an act of will; and each habit is thus a specialized form of volitional tendency, a special development of will. Every act of will is a pursuit of some good; and a habit is a special set, or tendency, of will to pursue certain particular goods as opportunity offers. The habit thus arises out of the general tendency of will to pursue the good — and the greatest good within its horizon. Thus the *individuality* or individual personality is a special set of volitional tendencies (forms of will) developed out of a general volitional tendency (a general will) to pursue the greatest possible good. And if the individual is to be a well integrated (or harmonious) personality his habits must be kept in harmony with each other and with the general will to the greatest good.

MIND, LIFE AND CONSCIOUSNESS

The individual mind, therefore, is a growth of special volitional tendencies that grow out of the general will to the good. But whence comes the general will to the good? The answer is that it is in every living thing that feels pleasure or pain, comfort or discomfort, or any other form of good or evil. It is that which struggles and strives in everything that struggles and strives; and it strives to increase the good in the experience of that creature. But in each creature its outlook, or knowledge, is limited to that of the creature. It is an active striving after the good, but with a finite or limited outlook.

It is this feeling and striving that distinguish the living from the nonliving. Even single-celled organisms like the amoeba give evidence of it. The consciousness that we enjoy is the unification of a mass of feelings, centered in the activity of the cells of the cortex of the brain. These feelings are held together by the act of attention. When we become sufficiently inattentive we become unconscious. The spotlight of attention is the height of consciousness, leaving a mass of vague feeling in the background that is marginally conscious, subconscious, and even unconscious. For the unconscious processes of life are not devoid of feeling and striving. A mass of evidence from abnormal psychology proves that.

Consciousness is a certain selected mass of present feeling of the living organism, pulled together and retained for a brief space of time. It enables us to distinguish the passage of time in the transition of feeling; and thus we become aware of the distinction of past and future. This makes recognition possible when the same kind of feeling recurs. And it makes learning possible as we discern the connection of different felt objects, one following another. This act of attention which pulls feelings together creates consciousness. Without it feeling and striving still exist, but unconsciously, because they are disconnected and momentary. We know that this is so because abnormal psychology has discovered an abundance of cases where people have later become conscious of past feelings and strivings of which they were not conscious at the time they occurred.

It may seem, at first, like a contradiction in terms to speak of " unconscious feelings." But a little reflection shows that consciousness requires much more than the existence of a present feeling. To be conscious we must also be able to hold that feeling in immediate memory when it has passed, connect it with the new present feeling, and anticipate some further feeling. Consciousness is a linking up of feelings into a connected whole which constitutes intelligible experience. This makes memory possible; and habits linked by memory constitute personality.

Abnormal psychology, however, shows us that, in any individual, this linking may be very incomplete. In the one individual there may be a set of linked feelings that are separate from the main body and constitute a secondary consciousness, a repressed personality. This is abnormal. But the normal consciousness certainly shuts out a mass of feelings, especially when it is most highly attentive. And some of these certainly seem to function as though they were interlinked in secondary conscious association. So it is evident that our nightly sleep and other gaps in normal consciousness do not indicate complete absence of feeling, or even complete cessation of all forms of secondary consciousness. We lose the connections whereby we remember or become aware of them. That is all.

The evidence, then, is fairly conclusive that will (i.e., feeling and striving) is continuous throughout life, present in every cell of a living organism, though it is not always gathered together in that act of attentive consciousness whereby the individual strives to direct the behavior of his organism as a whole. And this will, as we have seen, is always a striving after what is felt or anticipated as good.

The general will to the good can therefore be traced back to the beginnings of life. It was the activity that made the difference between the animate and inanimate in the first bit of living substance on earth. That activity was a response to a feeling of something good. It was a striving to maintain and increase that good. In course of time this striving built up what we call a living cell; and that cell grew and multiplied itself into many distinct cells. Thus the ongoing activity of the initial general will to the good developed special set forms (or habits) in each different organism, enhancing their powers and adapting them to a particular environment and mode of life. It developed the power of gathering up the multiple feelings of a cell into the beginnings of attentive consciousness, and so distinguished between before and after, and formed the capacity to learn by experience. In its special set forms it developed colonies of cells and organized these into a multicellular organism. It developed the organization of the attentive consciousness into an intelligent human mind, capable of thinking of the good of other selves.

Up to this point the outlook of this feeling-striving

process, as present in each organism, had been limited
to the good of that organism.   But now it became aware
of a vast range of other goods in the lives of other organisms.   And it then showed its true nature, as a will
to the *greatest* good, by reaching out to produce the greatest good on the whole, even though not the greatest good
of the particular person through which it worked.   Then
it found itself sometimes in conflict with the particular,
specialized forms of will, directed toward particular, special goods of the individual, which it had developed in
the past.

As the attentive consciousness of the individual pulled
together its specialized habits to direct the activity of the
self as a whole toward its own greatest good it found its
familiar habits in conflict with a new form of desire
within itself, a desire for the good of some other person.
But this desire was new only in that it was a desire for
the good of another self.   It was old — the very oldest
form of desire — in that it was desire for the greatest
good.   And as the oldest form of will, the very source of
all the others, it asserted its authority.   The attentive
consciousness could not pull itself together into a single
united will by subjecting this original and ultimate form
of will to the other forms that had been developed as its
instruments.

The strength of the special habits often was enough to
flout this new aim of the old, original form of will.   But
they could not integrate it in subjection to themselves.
If they flouted it the self remained divided against itself,
and pained, when it reflected, by a sense of something
wrong.   So the effort at reintegration must be made, the
effort of attentive consciousness to subject the special
habits to the will to the greatest good.   It was an effort

at self-integration that had to be made by the self as a whole. It was hard; and it had to be made often. With practice it grew easier. It can grow almost habitual. But what self succeeds in always maintaining that integration perfectly?

GOD AS FOUND WITHIN

This, in brief, is the story of life on earth. It finds the origin of life in an act of will, responding to a feeling of something good and seeking to produce more good. But it does not assume that that original act of will was aware of the end from the beginning. It does not assume a consciousness of any ultimate goal toward which it is working. The story merely takes life as it is found. Life is seen as a process striving, in spite of difficulties, to produce all the good it can, making mistakes, getting at cross purposes with itself and producing evil, but still striving to correct its errors and drive ever to produce more and greater good.

Obviously, the story thus far is incomplete. We want to know more about that original act of will that has been expanding and multiplying itself ever since in all the amazing forms of life and the still more amazing history of man. Could that act of will be the first? What was it that produced it? Is it only in man and the animals that a multiplicity of feeling-striving processes (or acts of will) ever are integrated by an act of attention to form consciousness? How is this activity of feeling, or will, related to the physical body?

These are questions to be examined later. But even with the material we have gathered thus far we can answer the questions raised at the beginning of this chapter. We saw that, for religion, God is, above all, the source of the moral law. We asked: Can we know of any authority for the moral law higher than that of man? Can we know what the moral law really is? Now we see the answers. The moral law is that every person should at all times seek to do the greatest possible good for all concerned. It is the Golden Rule which religion long has taught us. And the authority for it is so much above any man or body of men that it is the fundamental source of all earthly life, the will that animates all that breathes, that is active still in every man. And with this will that seeks in and through each of us the good of all we must make our peace and live in harmony or there can be no peace or harmony in our souls.

If this will to the greatest good, which is the source and ultimate guide of our lives, our Alpha and Omega, is rightly called " God," then we see God face to face. We know him more intimately than we know any other person. For we only look on the external face of another man; we merely guess at the life within him. But we look upon the actual will of God in operation (his inner soul) as we do upon our own. We see the essential nature of his will more clearly and simply than we do the complex nature of our own. For God is in us. He is a part of us. We are products of his activity, outgrowths of his life. And he is active still within us, guiding us, admonishing us, using us, cheering us with the sense of inner peace and strength when we are in harmony with him.

This is exactly the sort of knowledge of God that our greatest religious teachers have declared we have. " Blessed are the pure in heart: for they shall see God " (Matt. 5:8). " For it is God that worketh in you both to will and to do of his good pleasure " (Phil. 2:13).

" In him we live and move and have our being " (Acts
17:28) . " In him was life; and the life was the light of
men . . . which lighteth every man that cometh into
the world " (John 1:4, 9) .

This is the knowledge of God that we have by immediate acquaintance.   It should be enough to make us recognize the nature and authority of the moral law.   But
we want to know more about God than this.   Indeed
many will hesitate to use the name " God " for something, however important, that we find within ourselves,
unless we can show that it is more than just in ourselves.
But other facts about God must depend on inference.
They cannot be given in immediate experience as are
the will to the greatest good and the sense of obligation
or authority attaching to it: God as found within us.   We
must infer the rest from nature and history and the details of personal experience.   But all our knowledge is
like that — even our knowledge of the physical world
and other persons.   Something is given in immediate experience and the rest is inferred from its relation to other
data of experience.

In our study thus far we have already inferred that
what we find within ourselves as a will to the greatest
good is the fundamental form of will from which our
whole personality has developed, and that it is continuous with the first act of will, which was the dawn of life
on earth.   If we call this will " God " then we can say
already that God is creative, personal, good, immanent
in man, and the source of the moral law which bids us
love our neighbors as ourselves.   But we cannot be content with this.   We want to know more of God's relation
to us and to the world, of what he has done in history and
of the hopes he holds out to us for the future.

But " God is a Spirit." If this is so then our further knowledge of him must come through a study of spirit where we know it best. This, if there really is any such thing at all, should be in the life of man. So we pass to our next question: Has man a soul?

Has Man a Soul?

DEFINITIONS

ONCE AGAIN we had better begin by defining our terms, for the term " soul " has been used sometimes for the animal life, sometimes for the immortal element in man, sometimes for the higher mental, moral and aesthetic capacities, whether believed to be immortal or not. We shall use the term here for that part of man's life and mind which may be believed to survive the death of the body. The terms " spirit " and " spiritual " we shall use for all the life and mind of man which is above the level of the other animals, whether this is all immortal or not. Thus we can distinguish sharply between man's animal and spiritual tendencies. The term " life " will be used to refer to all activities or processes other than the merely physical, whether conscious or not. We shall see reason to believe that all these processes or activities are of the nature of feeling and striving, even when unconscious. Thus all " life " is also " mental." There is no distinction between life and mind. But we shall use the terms " mind " and " mental " to refer more particularly to those processes or activities which normally *can* be conscious, though they may become unconscious.

THE ORIGIN OF FEELING

If the distinctive feature of life is the feeling-striving process we call " will," then whence did it come? Some

46

scientists have speculated that it has been produced in some mysterious way by some minute material body. Within the slimy substance, floating in the shallows of the warm seas when the earth's crust was new, the ultra-violet rays of the sun synthesized many new and complex chemicals. Somewhere a new synthesis or mixture of these clung together in a new sort of lump or extra-large molecule which began to act in an extraordinary way. It ingested, digested and egested other chemicals. It built itself up. It multiplied its own kind by division, and these new individuals built up colonies of cells and eventually developed multicellular organisms. Somewhere in the course of this process, perhaps at the very beginning, some of these chemical processes produced feelings. The processes that tended to build up the organisms felt good; those that disintegrated it felt bad. Along with feeling came striving — striving to maintain the good feelings and be rid of the bad. Thus the striving of the organism tended to maintain and expand its life. At length the feelings developed consciousness and the conscious struggle for existence and expansion of power began.

This theory, of course, implies the ethic of self-interest. The striving process is produced by the organism and always strives to build it up and maintain it. It strives for the good of another only as a means to its own good. The falsity of this ethical conclusion immediately suggests the falsity of the whole theory.

But there are other objections to it besides this. If feeling and striving were not present from the beginning, then it is most extraordinary that the early forms of living thing should behave in such a highly purposive-looking manner as they do. To meet this objection many advocates of this theory accept the view that these factors must have been present and operative from the beginning of life. In this form the theory is more plausible. But it is still faced with the objection that it supposes that a world in which there was nothing but the push and pull of bits of lifeless matter could produce something so utterly different as feeling, with all its wealth of qualities — color, sound, pain, pleasure and all the rest.

The difficulty of believing that matter produces feeling becomes still greater when we inquire from the physicist what matter is. He tells us that it is composed of units of electrical energy organized into atoms. Each atom consists of one or more units of positive electricity (" protons ") surrounded by one or more units of negative electricity (" electrons ") ; perhaps also some neutral units (" neutrons "). At the center there is a compact mass composed of protons (if more than one) and neutrons (if any). Around this revolve the electrons, like the planets in a miniature solar system, and relatively just as far away from the center. So most of the atom is empty space. The various parts do not touch each other, nor do they touch the parts of other atoms. The most solid-looking piece of matter is chiefly empty space, the units of energy pulling and pushing each other across distances relatively enormous. This apparent action at a distance, in the structure of a piece of matter, is a mystery, as is the apparent action at a distance we call gravitation, which holds our solar system together.

Now a little thought soon shows that it cannot be these separated units of electricity themselves that possess feeling. How could the feelings of a multitude of such separate units be combined into a single perception except by the activity of some unifying agent beyond them? Further, how could a set of such isolated feelings be combined into the unity of consciousness? If our feeling were located in the electrons and protons it would have to consist of a multitude of separate, shifting spots.

THE REALITY OF SPACE

The reason for the persistent effort of materialistic speculation to depict the units of physical energy as the locus of feeling is that materialism has always thought of matter as *the only reality* and has defined matter as that which occupies space. And these units of energy are all that physics can find as occupying space. So they are regarded as the only reality; and therefore they must be the locus of feeling and consciousness.

But this conclusion misses the significance of what modern physics has to teach us. It is no longer possible to regard the ultimate units of physical reality as bits of solid stuff moving around in empty space. They are units of energy, not bits of stuff. Energy is motion, activity. Careful physicists tend to describe their ultimate units simply as " operations," which have to be defined in terms of the operations we perform in measuring them. Physics knows nothing more about them than how they change position relative to each other. Chemistry and physiology can go on to describe how the operations physics describes are correlated with the sensations we feel. That is all we know from these sciences.

But what is the space in which these physical operations occur? Is it nothing? Then these operations are connected by nothing, for there is nothing but space between them. Obviously, space itself must be *something*, a reality of some sort. It is then a reality that is everywhere. In it occur all the operations that make up the physical world, and all the feelings, strivings and other activities that make up our minds.

This gives us a hint to answer another question. What is it that operates? There can be only one answer that avoids sheer invention of some purely imaginative entity or stuff. It is space. Space itself, the reality that is everywhere, is active in the form of that great system of interrelated operations which we call the energy system of the physical world. That would explain the mystery of action at a distance, the law of gravitation and the cohesion of the atom.

THE RELATION OF BODY AND MIND

If space is a *reality* (not just nothing) it would help us, too, to explain the mystery of feeling and its relation to the physical processes of the nervous system. Colors, sounds, and other qualities such as warmth and pain occur in space. Probably all space has *some* quality and the qualities change according to the physical operations in each particular space. The physical operations — e.g., electrons and protons — are events in space that set up changing tensions across the intervening space that holds them together. And with these changing tensions there are correlated changes in the quality present in that space. Thus, when a nerve is stimulated and a chemical change takes place in a certain part of the brain, this is correlated with a change of the quality present there.

But what is the function of these qualities in the whole scheme of things? Surely they have some part to play; surely the colors and sounds, pleasures and pains, have some effect upon our behavior! Yet physics and chemistry can find no way in which they do affect physical processes. There is much about the chemistry of living cells that is not known. But all physicochemical processes, so far as they are understood, seem to operate without any effect upon them other than the effect they have on each other. Certainly it is hard to see how qualities like blue and red could push a molecule around or cause it to break up.

But here the conception of space as the agent that operates in all physical activity again comes to our rescue. Space must also be the agent that operates in all mental activities — in seeing red and blue, hearing sound, feeling pain, liking this, disliking that, striving to change this or that. If so we can understand how, when a new quality appears in a certain space in the brain (its appearance being due to a new nerve stimulus) and the mental act in that space changes from liking the former quality to disliking the new one, this change of mental activity, being really an activity of space itself, may affect the physical activity of the same space. It need not increase or decrease the total physical energy. It need not create a new electron or proton, nor destroy any, in order to do this. It may merely facilitate the process of chemical synthesis, or the release of energy from some molecule. It would simply be that the change from feelings of appetition to feelings of aversion, or vice versa, in a certain brain space has an effect upon the other (i.e., the physical) operations in that space. For both are operations of the same reality — the same space. This gives a very simple answer to the problem of the relation of body and mind.

THE STRUCTURE OF A MIND

This conception — that space, the omnipresent reality, is what operates in our mental activity — gives us a very workable conception of mind. It is a conception perfectly in harmony with our best psychological knowledge. We should not say that space is mind, merely because it performs mental activity. And it would be just as wrong to say that space is matter, merely because another set of its activities constitutes the physical world. A physical thing (an atom or a stone) is a particular, interrelated set of physical activities. Similarly, a mind is a particular, interrelated set of mental activities. The connection between the physical activities is what we call physical causation. The connection between the mental activities is memory and purpose.

But neither mind nor matter is a distinct substance or stuff. The physical universe and the whole historic course of life and mind are simply two distinctive sets of activity of the one omnipresent reality. Each set of activities has its own kind of inner relationship; one is the physical-causal; the other is that of memory-purpose. And the two sets of activity have their effect upon each other. For the physical activity presents qualities which the mental feels, likes or dislikes, and strives to change or increase or maintain. This response of liking and disliking, feeling and striving, then has its effect upon the course of physical events in the place where it occurs, e.g., in a human brain. A material thing is an organized system of physical activities of space. A life or mind is an organized system of mental activities of space.

Now consider more carefully the structure of a human mind. It is an organization of feeling-striving activities, or acts of will. And these acts are not actions of any physical thing, nor of any particular local thing, but of the omnipresent reality. This reality we know immediately in its character of extension, or space. But we now discover it to be full of all sorts of other amazing potentialities.

The mental act consists in purposively attending to something. The objects attended to can be distinguished as having various colors and other sensory qualities, various shapes and sizes, motion and resistance. These features we classify together as the characteristics of physical objects. But we can also attend to our own mental activities; and we distinguish these as feeling, striving, perceiving, thinking, liking, disliking, etc.

The liking and disliking involve attention to a peculiar set of qualities of a kind we have not yet mentioned. They may be classified together as *values* and include the unique element felt in pleasure, pain, joy, sorrow, beauty, ugliness and every other sort of good and bad. We are at first inclined to regard the value-quality as depending entirely upon the nature of the object; e.g., the color of the rose is beautiful and its smell pleasant. But a more careful examination shows that the value-quality felt depends upon our own mental activity. The same color seen in a connection that gives it another meaning may appear ugly; the same smell on another occasion may be unpleasantly strong for us. Further, the value-qualities are often directly associated with our mental activities. We enjoy doing what interests us. If we have set our heart upon a certain goal we enjoy doing the things that seem to bring it nearer. In fact we can lay down a general rule that value-quality tends to be felt when our purposive activity (or that of a sense organ) is working

harmoniously and successfully toward its goals; disvalue
is felt in frustration and failure.

It is not necessary that the goal should be explicitly
in mind in order to affect our value experience and thus
affect behavior. Ordinarily we tend to forget the distant
goal while we pay attention to the present means that has
been seen as a step towards it. Our will can become set
on one of these means as a subsidiary goal; and we can
then enjoy working towards this subsidiary goal, quite
forgetting its ultimate purpose. Often we pursue it too
far, to the injury of our ultimate purpose; and then we
experience the unpleasantness or bitterness of frustration. This fact, that an act of will that is forgotten can
still affect our value experience, making the activity feel
enjoyable and satisfying or otherwise, shows that when
an act of will is forgotten *it does not necessarily cease to
exist.* It does not have to be conscious. Once established it can remain as an unconscious *set* of the mind.
It then vaguely affects our value experience without our
quite knowing what makes us happy or sad.

A human mind, therefore, consists of a complex organization of forms of will, set upon certain goals, not
all of which are conscious at any one time. Indeed, only
a small part of mind is conscious. The rest consists of
set forms, operations of the omnipresent reality (or
space) that have, as it were, taken their stand, become
set, and so affect the value experience of that mind even
when it is not conscious of them. If it does become conscious of them it is aware of them as wants or desires, set
upon certain goals. But consciousness involves an act
of attention which links up a selected group of feelings,
strivings and set tendencies, giving some a special prominence and leaving others in the background. This at-

tention, giving a special prominence to some forms of will over others, brings about changes in the effect of the mental operations of the omnipresent reality (space) upon its physical operations in the same area, i.e., changes in the brain, and thus in bodily behavior.

But we can see now why we are not always conscious. The various set forms of will are so many special habits. So long as they remain the same the brain activity remains the same. Then occurs a new mental act of attention to the good by one of these forms of will, with liking or disliking of a certain object so as to want it changed. This effects a special new set of brain activity. But the nerve cells are fit for these special changes of activity only when they are freshly charged with potential energy and free from fatigue products. If mental activity tries to drive them when they are fatigued it experiences weariness, headache and frustration. So mental activity has formed the habit of giving the brain periodic rest. It becomes inattentive, inactive, unconscious; i.e., it goes to sleep. Similarly mental activity ceases immediately to disturb the brain when the brain is badly jarred, attacked by noxious drugs, or if the blood supply fails. It is the well established set, or habit, of the mind, perhaps inherited from its past ancestry, in such circumstances to become inactive, to relapse into unconsciousness. Thus the brain is given a chance to recover.

WHAT SURVIVES DEATH?

What happens to the mind if the brain never recovers, if it and the body disintegrate? For answer we have no clear and certain evidence. But, unless our whole interpretation of the facts is wrong, the mind need not cease to exist. If the mental activity is an operation of the

omnipresent reality, then a set form of will is a set form
of that reality. And a human mind is an integrated organization of such forms of reality. Every interest that
a personality has developed is a form of will, a set form
in the omnipresent reality. And a mind is a system of
interests. There is no reason why these interests should
not become active, and thus conscious, again. They certainly should do so if their object still exists and their
activity can have some effect in the realization of their
goals.

The whole question of whether a mind may live on,
after the death of the body, would therefore seem to depend upon the nature of its interests and the possibility
of their realization without the body. Interests in the
body and its achievements would necessarily become inactive. The whole mass of physical habits and desires
of the flesh would thus be lost. The minds of animals
and the animal interests of man must cease to operate
when the body dies. But a great range of other interests
of a well developed personality would remain.

Our value experience is determined, not by our relation to physical things, but by the interrelation of our
mental operations. So long as these were harmonious
life would be happy. The richness of that life would
depend upon the richness of the set of interests developed in things independent of the body. Beauty is experienced in the activity of imagination and could still
be pursued, though not in its familiar sensory forms.
But since all the world is full of qualities we would form
new habits of attending to these instead of attending only
to those associated with our sense organs.

Further, it should surely be possible to develop new

means of communication with other minds. In telepathy there is already evidence that this is possible when we become more interested in another personality than in our own sensations. This is very difficult so long as our habit is to attend to these as media of communication. But when the familiar sensations are gone this habit must disappear, new means of communication will be sought, and if they can be found the interest in other persons will again become active. But it will have to be a positive interest in their welfare or it will make for unhappiness. A selfish or antisocial interest would clash with the will to the greatest good of all concerned, which will still be the fundamental form of will in each person. Thus hatred and pride developed here may be expected to make a person unhappy hereafter, until they are overcome, while love will make for happiness.

Finally, the truth interest could still be active. The body as a means of investigation and information would be gone. But there would be personalities and their relations as subject of inquiry; the relation of personality to the world would open new channels for research; perhaps even some operations of the physical world itself may still be felt and investigated.

Memory should be carried with us into the next life, for the function of the brain is simply to present objects — qualities, shapes, motions, etc. Each object as presented is merely present, whether its presentation is due to the sense organs or to imagination. The mind must carry its own past experience with it, subconsciously, in order to see in the newly presented object something with which it is familiar, something *like* the experience of the past. The dependence of memory upon the brain would seem to be due to the normal mind's habit of attending only to what is presented to it by its body — the body and what it can achieve through the body being the original and ever dominant interest of the normal earthly life.

Thus the answer to the question of our chapter is that man begins to develop a soul as soon as he develops interests that do not depend upon his body for their fulfillment. The soul is an organized system of such interests. Man is not born with a soul. He grows it. Its growth is essentially a moral process and it is one in which human beings can help or hinder each other. The soul developed in this life is more or less rich in the range of its interests. It is more or less well integrated. If it is selfish, or involves hatreds, it is warped and is bound to suffer until it can overcome these tendencies. It will be free, after death, from the habits of the flesh, good and bad, but not from the effect these have had in determining the direction of its interests — proud, self-centered and vindictive, or genuinely concerned with the greatest good. Only the latter types of interest make for true harmony in the soul and therefore for happiness. But the soul, at death, has not finished growing. Death is the beginning of a new life, in which the soul will develop old and new social interests and interests in beauty and truth. Above all, it can go on growing in the knowledge of God and in the joy of working in harmony with his will.

THE MORAL ARGUMENT FOR IMMORTALITY

This conception of the future life is derived directly from an analysis of the nature of mind and its relation to the body. But the ground for faith in immortality is enormously strengthened when we approach the question from the standpoint of our knowledge of God. In the next chapter we shall show reason to believe that God is not merely a higher will and moral demand immanent in ourselves, but also a supreme and all-embracing Person with an eternal, conscious purpose. We shall see that there seem to be some limits to his power; yet the possibilities which the universe may contain are beyond our guessing. The course of the evolution of life on earth has revealed amazing new potentialities of the universe at every stage; and there is no reason to think this life has exhausted its resources. The power of God and the further possibilities of the universe would have to be small indeed if they could not provide fresh means of communication and development to minds such as ours will be when they have left the body behind. Perhaps they may provide opportunity for further development even of the lives of infants — a hope for which the merely psychological evidence provides no basis.

From a faith in the eternal power of God it is a short step to faith in immortality. For God as immediately known to us is a will to the production of the greatest possible good in the lives of persons. He wills the continued life and wholesome development of individuals. And his demand upon us is that we should pursue the same end. It cannot be that God makes a moral demand upon us which he does not himself observe. So we must believe that the whole eternal power of God, in accord with his eternal purpose (assuming the validity of the argument of our next chapter), is directed to the cultivation and development of finite personalities like ourselves. No substitute for such individual, personal immortality could meet the demands of the moral will,

And those demands will surely be met, for the moral will is God within us.

MORAL OBJECTIONS TO IMMORTALITY

Finally, something should be said in answer to the objections to the doctrine of immortality that have been made on moral grounds. The Communist charge that religion is " the opiate of the proletariat " has been urged particularly against the doctrine of immortality. It has been called a device of the ruling class to persuade the dispossessed to be content with their lot, promising " pie in the sky when you die " for those who remain faithful servants in this life. John Dewey and others have also urged that speculation about a future life only turns people's attention away from the problems of this life, and should therefore be avoided.

Now it may be admitted that designing people have sometimes made illegitimate use of religious truths. But this does not make a truth any less true. Further, such objections as Dewey urges are pertinent only against a conception of immortality that divorces the status in the future life entirely from behavior and achievements on earth. As has been shown in this chapter, the future life to which we look forward is one in which the higher developments of personality begun in this life will be continued. It therefore makes those higher developments all the more important.

The fact that a personality has eternal possibilities makes it all the more important to make the most of its initial stages in this life. Every act here acquires the greater significance by reason of its repercussions in eternity. Not only is the importance of the moral law en-

hanced, but the value of the principle of neighbor-love
is specially emphasized. True happiness hereafter depends upon cultivation of a personality in harmony with
the will to the greatest good. And everything that can
be done to assist the higher development of personality
in this life is a contribution to the enrichment of a life
that is eternal. The task of making the most of the opportunities of this life is rendered, not less significant,
but infinitely more so, by the recognition that the life
which we help or hinder by our activity is not limited to
threescore years and ten.

In particular, the right of the individual to freedom
of conscience, and therefore to freedom of information
and inquiry and freedom of speech, attains its full significance only when it is recognized that any attempt to
limit these freedoms may enslave and inhibit the development of an immortal soul. Any imposition of bad
conditions upon individuals or classes that warps their
spiritual development, puts temptation in their way,
causes them to do wrong, is a crime against the eternal.
It was this that Jesus had in mind when he said, " But
whoso shall cause one of these little ones which believe
on me to stumble, it is profitable for him that a great
millstone should be hanged about his neck, and that he
should be sunk into the depth of the sea " (Matt.18:6).

The Christian doctrine of the supreme value of the
individual soul thus lies at the basis of our liberties. It
teaches that all differences of race, station, physique,
mentality, color or sex are insignificant compared to the
fact that a human being is an immortal soul, responsible
for himself directly to God, and a child of God whom
God loves. Those who think that the social status of the

humbler classes of men on earth could be advanced by the abandonment of faith in immortality have completely failed to grasp the significance of this faith in the course of history. It is one of the great pillars on which has always rested the democratic doctrine of the dignity of man.

What Is God Like?

GOD IN US AS WILL, NOT IDEA

WITH THE understanding of the nature and destiny of man developed in the last chapter we are in a better position to understand the nature of God and his relation to man. We see the whole course of life on earth as beginning and ending with God, and God as present and active all the way through. As we have already seen, we know God immediately as active within ourselves — a will to the greatest good of all concerned that asserts its moral authority over all our other desires. This will, however, as it operates in us, does not at first carry with it a clear consciousness of its own end. It is impossible that it should; for the very young child is not aware of the existence of other selves as centers of experience separate from his own. We cannot pursue the good of others until we are aware of their existence. So the divine will in us pursues the greatest good that is seen and recognized as greatest by each individual mind. The individual mind may fail to see some possibilities of good; it may make mistakes as to which is greatest. But the divine will in us establishes a desire and a sense of obligation to be true to the *greatest,* even if it is a good for some other person but not for ourselves.

This view is perfectly in harmony with the opening verses of the Gospel of John: " In the beginning was the

Word, and the Word was with God, and the Word was God. The same was in the beginning with God. All things were made by him; and without him was not anything made that was made. In him was life; and the life was the light of men. . . . That was the true light, which lighteth every man that cometh into the world."

This text has been much misunderstood by theologians because the Greek word *logos,* which means " mind," " reason," " thought " or " word " and is here translated " Word," is connected in Greek philosophy with Plato's notion of certain perfect " ideas " which are eternal objects of the divine mind. So it has been suggested that the " light which lighteth every man that cometh into the world " is a certain set of perfect moral ideas. Thus the human conscience was thought to be a sort of instinctive knowledge of what is right — " the voice of God within us," telling us exactly what we should do. Against this interpretation many people pointed out that conscience makes many mistakes and so its ideas cannot be the voice of God.

Now what our analysis of the structure and development of the human mind shows us is that God is in us as a *will* to pursue the greatest good, not as an *idea* of what is the greatest good. Our intelligence has to find *what* is good. And the good changes so, with changing circumstances, that it is impossible to lay down any absolutely rigid rules. Conscience is indeed " the voice of God within us " in so far as it demands that we try to find out what is the greatest good possible in every situation and strive to produce and maintain it. If we set aside our prejudices and favoritisms conscience will always demand this. But it is a great mistake to think that any particularly strong and vivid idea of what is right in a certain situation (which is what is ordinarily meant by conscience) is the voice of God.

The words in John's Gospel would seem to agree with this view. The word *logos* in most Greek philosophy meant much more than a perfect idea. And it means much more for the Gospel writer. It is a creative power and life. It is the " life " that is " the light of men." And life, while it may have ideas, is much more, and may exist without them. It is primarily feeling and striving, i.e., will. The *logos,* if we use that term, is the creative will, feeling and striving after the good as it feels and sees it. In that process it has developed all the forms of life. Each one seeks the good; but each one has a limited vision; it can err and produce evil and destroy greater goods than it produces.

It is therefore correct to say that all the forms of life are created by God and that God is in them all. But it is not correct to say that each is and does exactly what God, from the beginning, planned it should be and do. That conception of God would make him directly responsible for all the evil of the world. God did not specifically plan either the sweetness of honey, or the sting of the adder, or the misery of disease. God, in his activity in animate nature, seeks the good in and through each living thing as it is seen from the standpoint of that living thing, not as it is seen from some all-inclusive standpoint that sees and knows all things, planning every detail from beginning to end.

INFINITE MIND AND FINITE MINDS

This does not mean that there is in God no higher consciousness, no eternal plan. A mind with an eternal consciousness and an eternal plan might well initiate a growing, creative process, which would be beyond its direct control in detail and yet would, as a whole and in the long run, fit into the eternal plan — a plan which might well provide for the continuous development of relatively independent individuals within the whole.

This is exactly what is suggested by our analysis of the structure and development of mind. We have traced the life and mind of man back to an initial act of will which found on this planet conditions that made possible a new kind of constructive activity, with almost infinite possibilities of varied development. These conditions, combining water, earth and air with a certain narrow range of temperature variations, astronomers tell us are a very rare phenomenon. Probably they exist nowhere else in the universe, unless it be on our sister planet, Mars. However that may be, when these new forms of physical activity appeared in space, space (the reality that is everywhere) responded to them. The response was a constructive interest in the new physical forms and qualities. The resulting experience felt good so long as it was successfully constructive. It felt bad when the result of activity was disintegration of the new structure and thus a disappointment of the constructive interest. Thus the process of interested, vital activity went on — a process of attentive feeling and striving, building up a new form of body that could maintain itself, grow and multiply itself.

Now any single interest-process is absorbed in its own object. It does not of itself involve a memory of the purposive act that initiated it, nor of the ultimate goal which that act may have in view. For example, a student writing an essay has to look up a certain fact in a book. He takes up the book to search for the fact.

Presently he is absorbed in the interest of reading the book. He has forgotten the purpose for which he took the book up. Something must occur to bring his attention back to this original purpose or it would be forgotten altogether. The new interest goes ahead, oblivious of its origin.

Something like this must have occurred in the initiation of the creative process of life on earth. Assuming that there is an eternal conscious mind, with an eternal purpose, this mind would see the opportunity for creative activity and development of new individual lives on this planet. It would react with constructive, interested attention to the new situation. This act would be an act of will (feeling and striving) seeking to control the new physical form in ways felt as good, and going on to develop new forms and new goods, always the greatest possible good. The new interest-process would be aware of its own object, the physical form and quality, and would strive to maintain and increase what it there found as good. It would manifest adaptive reaction and persistency with varied effort. But it would have no surviving consciousness of the act of will that initiated it, nor of the ultimate purpose held by the mind that performed that act of will.

The originating mind could be aware of the new interest-process, and of the goal it was intended to pursue, and of its success or failure. But the creative interest-process itself would be absorbed in its own object, unaware that it was a part of a larger mind. It would thus become a new and independent individual, a life with its own body, gradually developing as a distinct center of consciousness.

In a mind that has only one distinct body through

which to express itself, it is a mistake and a failure to let any single interest-process get beyond control of the originating center of consciousness. But an eternal consciousness would have a multitude of distinct bodies through which to express itself. And its purpose would be to produce independent, individual minds, which could develop a range of unique experiences to enrich the experience of the universal mind. In particular, the development of independent, individual minds would make possible the creation of a unique range of values, the social values, including love. Love can be experienced only when there are two or more relatively independent minds. And if there are two or more minds only one of them can be infinite (embracing all experience). The others must be limited, finite, or they would be identical. Being finite these other minds must be independent, erring, and sometimes opposed to the will of their creator. But that is the price even God must pay for having other individuals, with independent minds, to love.

If there is an eternal, conscious mind with an eternal purpose, and if it was this mind that initiated the process of creative activity of life and mind which we call the course of evolution and of human history, then our minds are specific interest-processes within the universal mind, working more or less in harmony with the purpose for which we were created. The universal mind could be aware of us and share our consciousness, though we could not share his.

We must not assume, however, that the relation between our mind and the universal mind (if there is such) would be exactly the same as that between a single interest-process and the human mind in which it occurs.

Our minds are much more complex than any single interest-process and have bodies of their own, a fact which gives them a much greater independence. Another analogy would be that of such free-moving bodies as the white corpuscles of the blood stream, which live much like independent organisms and yet are an organic part of a larger organism. Another analogy, suggesting a still greater independence, is that of parent and children. No analogy is perfect. All are misleading in some respects. But of this we can be sure, that if our minds are the product of the activity of a larger mind, then there must remain some sort of organic relation between them.

POSSIBILITY OF AN ETERNAL CONSCIOUSNESS

It is time to face the main question. Is there a larger mind than our own from which all life and mind have sprung? Is God, as known within us and active in the whole development of life from its inception, an agency that had its first beginnings with the first act of will which constituted the first throb of terrestrial life? Or was that first act of will the conscious act of a mind that existed beforehand?

We have already seen reason to believe that qualities more or less akin to those that we feel in sensation are properties of space, the omnipresent reality. They are not the special creation of the molecules of our brains, but are displayed everywhere. We have also seen that it is space that feels and strives, not the molecules of the brain. It would be most extraordinary, therefore, if a reality that is *capable* of feeling the changing variety of qualities that everywhere flow through it should never have felt anything until a few thousand years ago on earth. It would be strange, too, if a reality that is capable, in small individual organisms, of attending to its feelings in such a way that it becomes conscious should practice this attention only in those organisms.

In brief, once we have recognized that it is space, the omnipresent reality, that feels and is conscious, not just certain minute units of physical energy, there is little reason for thinking that feeling and consciousness do not exist until physical energy has developed the special forms or organization with which *our* consciousness is associated.

Some say that while it is possible that there is an eternal mind, there being no evidence against it, yet there is no evidence for it. They claim that it is just as plausible to think that feeling and consciousness originated along with the development of the nervous system as to think that they are an eternal feature of reality. They are willing to swallow the implausibility that a reality capable of consciousness should have remained unconscious until awakened by certain minute changes in the structure or arrangement of certain molecules; or they choose to believe that these minute changes made that reality capable of consciousness even though it was not capable of it before.

In saying that there is no evidence *for* an eternal consciousness these thinkers are looking for evidence of the wrong sort. *Our* consciousness is concerned with the special purposive behavior of a particular body, directing it to certain special goals and adapting it to special circumstances. Those who say there is no evidence of consciousness outside of human and animal life mean that there is no evidence of such special adaptive behavior of anything outside of human and animal life. Nature does not modify her laws in order specially to adapt herself to human needs or to reward human beings according to their desert.

But should we expect that an eternal consciousness would manifest itself in special adaptations of natural laws to human needs? What ground is there for believing that feeling and striving could have such effects as would be recognizable as special changes in the natural order made for a moral purpose? So far as our evidence up to this point goes, feeling and striving have no effect upon the course of physical events except to facilitate or retard certain chemical changes in some of the very unstable carbon compounds of living cells. This implies some very slight effect upon the operations of physical energy. In the delicately balanced structure of a living organism a very slight effect upon certain nerve changes may make a great difference in behavior. In the long-run course of the physical world, spread over the immensities of space and time, the influence of a universal world-mind may also be great. But there is no evidence from mind as we know it to suggest that an eternal and universal consciousness would be able to work miracles for man's special benefit, enlightenment or punishment.

EVIDENCES OF DESIGN

Is there, then, any evidence of the long-run influence of mind upon the course of the physical world? Yes, it can be found in two facts. The first is the almost universal predominance of beauty over ugliness in nature. Beauty and ugliness are two distinct possibilities in the arrangement of material things. If the universe were a chaos it might be expected to throw up the one as often as the other. But almost everywhere it is beautiful.

Nearly all the ugliness is made by man. Inanimate nature is never ugly. Even deserts, ice floes, oceans, storms and volcanoes are beautiful, however uncomfortable and destructive they may be to human flesh. Animate things in nature are rarely ugly, though often unpleasant or dangerous to man.

Animate nature, however, is the product of myriads of special, adaptive feeling-reactions of living things, and must therefore be much less subject to the long-term influence of the eternal consciousness. Yet some such long-term influence in favor of beauty must have been operative here too. For it is very easy for the shortsighted feeling and striving reactions of living things to create ugliness — as man discovers as soon as he starts to interfere with nature and build cities. Since it is so easy to produce ugliness it is difficult to escape the conclusion that the vast predominance of beauty in nature must be due to the design of some higher mind.

The validity of this argument is not affected if beauty is regarded as merely subjective, i.e., merely a product of the mind perceiving it. The argument simply points to the fact that nature is such as to affect human minds predominantly with an experience of beauty. It may be that nature is marvelously adapted to have this effect upon mind. Or it may be that mind is marvelously adapted to receive this effect from nearly all the various forms of nature. In either case the adaptation is equally marvelous and indicates a long-run designing influence in favor of beauty, for beauty has no survival value for the struggling animal, and random, undesigned activity most commonly produces ugliness.

A second evidence of the influence of design in the universe is the peculiar adaptation of our earth and solar system to its function as the medium for the development of rational, moral individuals. To say this is not to argue that this is " the best of all possible worlds," that " whatever is is best," that everything is made by God for a special purpose and exactly fulfills his will. Traditional theology, with its theory of special creation, made God directly responsible for all the evils of nature. But this ascription of responsibility was due to the inadequacy of ancient science. Primitive philosophers, lacking any knowledge of the laws of physics and biology, borrowed an idea from religion to fill the gaps in their knowledge of the world. Religion had developed the conviction that the moral law is determined and upheld by a mysterious superhuman power. So the primitive philosopher assumed that this same superhuman power must be the explanation of all the mysteries of nature — the movement of sun, moon and stars, the change of the seasons, the reproduction of life, the origin of all things. This theory of special creation still survives in religious thought today, in spite of our knowledge of physical laws and evolution. It is responsible for much trouble to religious minds, who wonder why God should have produced a world so full of evil.

But in our study of the relation of mind and matter we saw reason to believe that the direct influence of mind upon matter is very small. And we have seen no reason to believe that an eternal and universal consciousness would have any greater influence at any one place and time. We therefore should not expect miracles. Nor should we expect the world to be adapted in every detail to our comfort and convenience. The long-range influence of the eternal consciousness, working out its long-range plan, has been able to provide at least one place in the universe where finite minds, developing their own individuality from a single act of will, could find a medium of expression in constructive control of some of the processes of the physical world. So far as we know, this is the only way in which finite, individual, independent minds could be developed. They cannot be constructed as mature and complex entities all at once, but must begin with the single, minimal act of feeling and striving, and must grow by their own efforts. We may assume that if there were a better way the eternal consciousness would have chosen it.

It is not difficult to see what are the requirements for the development of a rational, moral individual. There must, in the first place, be a medium that the individual can control, some kind of material with which he can work. This material must react upon his feelings according to regular natural laws, so that he can learn to anticipate its reactions. Only a world of natural laws is a possible home for rational beings. The reactions of the material must, further, give him satisfactions, so as to encourage further efforts on his part. But they must also present him with problems, difficulties in the way of satisfaction, or he would never think, never develop his mind. So life must have some possibilities of dissatisfaction and disappointment. Finally, he must be able to become aware of other minds and create a society. This sets before him the moral demand to concern himself with the good of others besides himself and also opens up to him that vast new range of values found in society, especially those found in love. If individuals are to know love and moral responsibility they must be to some extent dependent on each other, bringing joy and sorrow upon each other as well as themselves and sharing joy and sorrow with each other.

Now this world is not perfectly adapted to our comfort and convenience; but it meets the above requirements and serves very well its main function as a medium and a stimulus for the development of rational moral individuals. Some religious thinkers argue that it serves this purpose so well that, after all, we are entitled to think that it is perfectly adapted to God's purpose and that God is absolutely all-powerful, able to introduce any change at any moment into the laws of nature, but wisely refraining because it is better for us to be left to solve our problems for ourselves. This, however, is carrying the conclusion much further than the evidence warrants. It is even against the evidence.

It cannot be shown that the amount of pain in the world is all morally necessary. On the other hand, it is our duty to reduce suffering; and in general we find that people are morally better if we can succeed in reducing suffering or fending it off from them. It cannot be to our moral good to suffer from evils that we have not the knowledge or power to avoid, however good we may be. The evils of tornadoes, floods and earthquakes fall on guilty and innocent alike; and there is no evidence that the inhabitants of areas thus affected are better or worse than others. Disease is, in part, a moral problem, but much more a scientific one. As science saves us from disease we are not made morally worse. It is evident from all these considerations that the order of the physical world cannot be regarded as perfectly adjusted to man's animal and spiritual needs. Some features of the physical world must therefore be regarded as beyond the immediate control of a God who wills for man all possible good.

Now our knowledge of the relation of body and mind suggests that, though the long-range influence of mind on matter may be great, and though upon certain delicate organizations of matter a single mental act may have decisive results, yet the immediate influence of mind upon matter in general, outside of living cells, is negligible. This, it would seem, would exactly explain the great but imperfect extent to which the earth is adapted to the habitation of man. We have already mentioned the fact that this planet is believed by astronomers to be perhaps the only place in the universe, besides Mars, suitable for life as we know it. All the rest of the stars and their satellites are much too hot or too cold, lack air or water or other necessities of plant and animal life. Our solar system is apparently due to an " accident " in the history of the sidereal universe which seems to be extraordinarily rare and perhaps absolutely unique. Yet without it the universe (if there is no eternal consciousness) would have carried all its potentialities of life and mind, joy and beauty, forever unrealized. It is difficult indeed to believe that so extremely rare an event, fraught with such momentous consequences, could really be an accident. Yet if there is an eternal consciousness, able to exercise a very slight but continuous influence upon the course of the physical world, its long-range, planned activity could well be understood as the cause of that rare event.

Thus we can see the working of the eternal mind in the preparation of our earthly home, as well as in the creation of finite life. The eternal mind is responsible for the beauty of the universe and for the general adaptation of this planet to the needs of our lives, but not for all the details of its structure, nor for all the forms of development of life. The world of inanimate and animate nature is one for which we must be grateful to God. But it is not entirely shaped according to his will or ours. To some extent we can work with him to improve it. But we must accept the fact that there is little in the course of nature that even God can immediately change.

In answer, then, to the charge that there is no evidence of the existence of an eternal consciousness we can say, first, that we have no right to look for evidence in the form of miracles, because these are beyond the reach of any power that we have reason to believe an eternal consciousness would possess. Second, that in the predominance of beauty in nature, and in the preparation of the earth to be a home and medium for the development of finite individual minds, we have strong evidence of the only kind that we have a right to expect.

CAN THE UNCONSCIOUS PRODUCE CONSCIOUSNESS?

In addition to these evidences of the operation of an eternal consciousness upon the order of the physical world, the very existence of finite consciousness on earth is evidence of the existence of an eternal consciousness. Either there must be an eternal consciousness or the production of consciousness on earth is a miracle — and a miracle occurring without even a God to perform it. Obviously no scientific and rational mind should believe in such a miracle.

A miracle is an event — something happening in the course of time — without the sort of antecedents that could explain it as part of the regular causal order. The eternal existence of matter and natural law would not be a miracle; nor would the eternal existence and operation of feeling and consciousness; nor the normal, minimal influence of consciousness upon the physical world exercised in favor of beauty or in bringing about the " accident " that produced our earth; nor the natural behavior of life on earth. All these things constitute the nature of matter and mind and are in accord with their regular functioning. But, if the eternal consciousness should exercise an influence upon physical events that is beyond the regular effect of mind upon matter (due to their both being operations of the one omnipresent reality, space), that would be a miracle. If a finite mind should exert such an *irregular* effect upon matter it would be a miracle. Similarly, if matter should exert an effect upon mental activity other than the effects it produces in the *regular* causal order, that would be a miracle.

Now matter, as we have seen, affects mental activity through the changing qualities of space (color, sound, smell, warmth, etc.) which are correlated with the changing tensions of physical events in space. Physical changes produce qualitative changes. New physical arrangements present new sensory qualities. But sensory qualities are not mental activities. The mental activities are the *feeling* of the physical events and the qualities of space associated with them, the *striving* to maintain or change these qualities and physical processes, the *liking* and *disliking* them, *attending* to them and to other mental activities, *expecting* or *anticipating* new ones, *recognizing* some as familiar, *noticing* and *thinking* about the relations between them.

If consciousness is not eternal, then either it came into being without a cause or it was caused by what existed before it. If it came into being without a cause that certainly was a miracle. So let us see whether it could have

been caused by the regular (i.e., nonmiraculous) operation of the factors that might have existed before it.
These would be the physical operations of space, with
their changing qualities, and probably feeling and striving, since it seems possible for these latter to occur unconsciously. Consciousness, as we have seen, involves an
act of attention to two or more processes of feeling and
striving in their relation to each other and to physical
events, qualities and other mental activities. It is an
act that holds these together so that passage of time is no-
ticed and memory and expectation are made possible.
Our question is, therefore, whether this new act of attention could be caused by the regular operation of the
physical activities, qualitative changes, and unconscious
feelings and strivings, which may be supposed to have
preceded it.

When the question is asked this way it is apparent that
the answer is " No." The *regular* operation of physical
changes produces only other physical changes. New
physical changes are all produced in accord with natural
laws, but they are simply new spatio-temporal relations
of the old units of physical energy — not new kinds of
activity, like an act of attention. They are correlated
with new physical qualities (color, etc.) which may or
may not become objects of feeling. But this feeling
would be an act of the same kind as other feelings, only
the kind of quality felt being new. So if previous feelings were unconscious this would be too. If all feeling
were conscious, but consciousness not eternal, then feeling would not be eternal. That would merely shift the
problem back to where this conscious feeling began. We
would have to suppose that some slight change in arrangement of physical energy produced both feeling of

qualities and consciousness of these feelings at the one moment. And this would be still more miraculous.

In brief, the production of consciousness by unconscious processes would be a sort of causal production that science cannot logically admit. Supporters of the theory of " emergent evolution " are mistaken in thinking that it is simply analogous to the emergence of new forms of physical things and organisms. These, as they point out, present new qualities to our senses and manifest new modes of physical activity which result in new effects upon other things. This sort of emergence of new things and organisms is explicable (at least theoretically) in terms of the regular causal relations of physical events and the normal process of qualitative change accompanying physical change. But this analogy breaks down when we remember that mental activity is not a quality and that it is uniquely different in kind from physical activity. And conscious mental activity is uniquely different from unconscious feeling. It is a distinctive process of attention, interested in a different kind of object, superimposed upon feelings which may otherwise be unconscious, but not derived from them.

The only way, therefore, to avoid a hypothesis that would involve the unscientific and irrational notion of a miracle happening by accident is to recognize that consciousness must be eternal. The act of will which initiated the life process on earth was the act of a conscious and eternal mind. It was an interest in creative activity that would develop new forms of both body and mind. The first product of the creative act was the initiating of a process of feeling and striving which had to work first with a minimum of that attentive interrelation of feelings we call consciousness. Perhaps it — the first and simplest form of life — was conscious only in flashes; perhaps not at all. But the original act of conscious interest established a " set " of the will which produced that attentive process we call consciousness as occasion offered, and developed at length into the multiple forms of conscious life we know.

THE ETERNAL CONSCIOUSNESS AND THE SOURCE OF THE MORAL LAW

That set form of will, thus imparted to the stream of life at its inception, and passed on to every living organism, makes every act of feeling-striving a striving to maintain and produce what is felt as the greatest present good and anticipated as the greatest possible future good. Thus, when the organism becomes aware of possibilities of good outside its own immediate experience, it strives to produce them as it does its own. And when the greatest possible good is seen as a good of some other person which can be realized only by sacrifice of some lesser good of the self, it still demands that the self should pursue that greatest good. Thus that fundamental form of will imparted to all life by the eternal consciousness becomes, in man, a demand felt within him that he concern himself with the good of others equally with the good of self.

At this point, therefore, we are able to link up the knowledge obtained through analysis of our religious and moral experience with that obtained in this analysis of the interrelation of mental and physical activity. We are able to identify the eternal consciousness, which we find to be implied by the nature and history of mind and matter, with the superhuman source of the moral experience. Without this identification the existence of an eternal consciousness would have no religious or moral significance. What would it matter to us to know that our consciousness is derived from and shared by a universal and eternal consciousness if we could not know that that consciousness wills our good and seeks in and through us the good of all?

But it makes a great difference to our religious and moral outlook to know that the power we find in us as source and sanction of the moral law is eternal, constantly conscious of us and interested in our welfare. Even though we see that we cannot expect the special intervention of the eternal, conscious agent in our favor in control of natural events, this knowledge gives us confidence that our spiritual welfare is safe in his care. We can look to him with thankfulness for the beauty of the world, and for the provision of our earthly home to supply our needs in accord with intelligible natural laws. We can see that the evils of the world are beyond his immediate control, but that his will is with us to strengthen us in all our efforts to overcome them. We can know that the will that seeks the greatest good of all is the eternal part of us, that the evil, in the long run, must die, but that all that is good in the spiritual part of the personality we build shall live eternally.

OMNIPOTENCE AND THE TRINITY

We have arrived at this conception of God through an analysis of moral and religious experience in the light of modern scientific knowledge. Let us now compare it with the traditional conceptions of Christian theology; we shall find the differences are not very great.

In our view God is a person; indeed he is the only complete person, for he includes all others and they are

WHAT IS GOD LIKE?

rooted and grounded in him. A human person is an interrelated set of physical and mental activities of a part of space. The personality of God includes the whole of space and the whole range of physical and mental activities. Just as our person includes some semi-independent organisms, living their own life and not always entirely in harmony with the good of every other part or with our will, so does the person of God. But though evil is possible within his being his *will* is always good, always willing the greatest good of all, and therefore morally perfect. He is omniscient in the sense that he has all the knowledge that exists. For all knowledge occurs in him and he shares the consciousness of all his creatures. He is not all-powerful in the sense of being able to do *anything*. Every theology has had to recognize that some things are at least logically or morally impossible to God. We have to go further and say that many things are also physically impossible. But he is all-powerful in the sense that he includes all the power that exists in the universe. There is no power beyond his. He is also infinite in the sense that he is not limited by anything beyond himself. There is no being beyond him.

Christianity has also said that God is three persons in one, the Father, the Son (identified with the Logos, or eternal mind), and the Holy Spirit. The reason for this tripartite conception of God lies in religious experience. Man feels God within him; that is the Holy Spirit. The Christian sees a perfect life in Christ, concludes that he was divine, and identifies his life and mind with that of the eternal. But philosophical thought sees that its God must be more than either an eternal mind or a moral power in man. So it frames the final conception of God the Father as the inclusive source and sustainer of all. It is then recognized that in each of these concepts God is personal. So he must be three persons. Then to save the unity of God these three persons are said to be " of one substance."

Now the difficulty in this conception has come from the traditional notion of a person as a separate soul, and of the soul as a single separate piece of substance, having its own absolutely private consciousness. How, on this view, could the Holy Spirit be a single person inside every human person? How could the three divine persons be one substance? These problems disappear when we learn the true nature of personality. If we are to speak of " substance " there is only one in all the universe. That is space. And a " person " is simply a special, organized set of the activities of space. These sets of activities can be organically related to each other, so that one person can be an organic part of another. And since consciousness depends upon a special act of attention within a personality there may be different levels of consciousness within the one person. We thus have no difficulty in seeing how God can be in man, and man in God, and how yet God and man, in each instance, can be distinct persons. And all are gathered up in the one supreme and universal person.

Christian theology, in the doctrine of the trinity, has attempted to give a true account of God as known in religious experience and thought. But it had to try to do it in terms of the inadequate and inaccurate concepts developed by Greek philosophy. Modern scientific philosophy gives us more accurate concepts and more adequate terms by means of which we can make the matter clear. We thus see that the ancient theologians, who distinguished between God the Father and the Holy Spirit, were justified in what they tried to express, even though the terms and concepts they had to use made it impossible for them to avoid apparent contradiction. In a later chapter we will inquire how far they were justified in speaking of Jesus as God the Son.

Is God Revealed in History?

PROPHETIC INSIGHT AND RELIGIOUS PROGRESS

WE HAVE seen reason to believe that God, the super-human source and sanction of the moral law, is not only within us, but that we are also in him. He is the supreme Person. His mind is eternally conscious and incomprehensibly complex. It includes in its organized wholeness all finite minds, all finite consciousness, all finite knowledge. The physical universe is a nonmental and nonvoluntary phase of the systematic activity of his being. It and all its changing qualities are an object of his attention. In its orderly but slightly malleable nature it is a medium of expression of his mind. Our minds are the offspring of his, but offspring that remain, as it were, within the parental womb, never leaving to live an entirely independent life, yet having something of the freedom of children. We are branches of the eternal Vine, yet sons of the eternal Father.

It was not through philosophizing about the natural world that men arrived at this conception of God as the True Vine and the Eternal Father. It is not a new conception. It has been gradually hammered into shape by those who have given thought to the moral and spiritual life. It has been developed in a series of deep spiritual insights by the great prophets and teachers of the Hebrew-Christian tradition. And in the best of the non-Christian religions a very similar view of God has been

86

similarly developed. In the early stages of this development there were errors and inadequacies that have been corrected and filled out at later stages. At every stage the religious interpretation has had to fit itself into the rest of the body of human knowledge — the common-sense knowledge of the environment, together with whatever science and history were available.

Any scientific and historical errors thus creeping into the interpretation have had to be corrected as scientific and historical knowledge increased. False suggestions due to scientific and historical ignorance have even distorted the religious interpretation, as, for example, in the theory of the special creation of every distinct form of life, good and evil. Religion has had to wait for scientific advance to help it free itself from these errors. But the main advance of the religious interpretation itself — the development of the ideas of God, of the moral law, of man's origin, destiny and relation to God — has not come from the logical reasoning of scientifically minded philosophers. It has come from the poetic, passionate and devotional insights of the great religious prophets.

What then is the nature of these prophetic insights? Are they insights of the human spirit, pondering the problems of the spiritual life, fallible, yet progressively seeing the truth more and more clearly? Or are they special communications from the divine and eternal consciousness, given progressively to those who are able to understand and use them?

GOD'S REVELATION AND MAN'S DISCOVERY

On the former view, both the degree of progress and the degree of error depend entirely on three human factors: first, the amount of intelligent thought given to the problems by human beings; second, the historical circumstances and the more or less accurate historical knowledge and scientific ideas that pose the problems and suggest solutions, some true, some false; third, the degree of open-mindedness, or special prejudice, with which the facts are faced and suggested interpretations received. These factors may blind or deceive the thinker, or open up to him great new truths. But errors lead to difficulties. These drive some men to further thought. Thus gradually errors are corrected and progress made. But all the way through, on this view, the advance of religious knowledge is a human achievement. It does not depend on special communications from God.

Yet the absence of special communications does not mean that man's progressive discovery of religious truth is not in any sense a divine revelation. Without the active presence of God within him man could never come to know God. God reveals himself to man's inner consciousness as the sun reveals itself to his eyes. It is a revelation not of words but of deeds, not of ideas but of will. As the activity of the sun in shining impresses itself on our senses, so the activity of the will of God within us impresses itself upon our inner consciousness, convicting us of sin, revealing to us the divine nature as righteousness and love, a power and authority transcending that of man. But, as we must open our eyes to see the sun, and take careful observations in order to understand it and anticipate its movements, so we must open our eyes, spiritually, to see God, and make careful observations in order to understand his will.

It is the *will* of God that is directly revealed to us.

And in the last analysis it is only the will of God that we need to have directly revealed. If we do his will we do right and we can trust him for the rest. And his will is plainly revealed. We have only to rid ourselves of our prejudices to see it — the will to the good of all. Seeing it, and recognizing the obligation to be true to it, presents no intellectual difficulty. It does not require external communication. The difficulty is moral, created by the narrowness and selfishness of our habits, traditions and natural impulses.

THE INNER WITNESS

If a truth about God is communicated to us, from whatever source, it can carry justifiable conviction only if it is corroborated by the immediate knowledge of God as he is revealed to us within. If our hearts are closed to the inner revelation the outer also will be rejected. " If they have believed not Moses and the prophets," said Jesus, " neither will they believe, though one should rise from the dead " (Luke 16:31). Even a miracle could not convince people that an idea comes from God unless they felt it confirmed by what they know of God in their own experience. People who can believe in miracles can believe that they are performed by devils as easily as that they are performed by God. So faith comes only when " the witness of the spirit " within, as theologians call it, bears testimony to the truth of a doctrine first heard from without.

As with an external communication that comes from some prophetic teacher, so with any communication that might come from the eternal consciousness directly to the mind of the prophet. How should he know that it comes from God unless God, as directly known to him, bears witness to it? Dreams, visions, voices and persistent ideas bring all sorts of false and weird thoughts. They are much less reliable than logical inductions from ordinary experience. All the paraphernalia of extraordinary psychological phenomena are entirely lacking in evidential value. The prophets and people of ancient times can be excused for thinking that such experiences indicated the activity of some sort of supernatural beings, whether God, angel or devil. But abnormal psychology has explained these things too fully for us any longer to see in them evidence of special divine communication.

These considerations force upon us the recognition that ultimately the only source of God's revelation of himself to man is the activity of the divine will within us. For no idea, however it comes to us, can be recognized as a communication from God unless it is corroborated by that " witness within." This means, further, that no special communication or special revelation can reveal to us more of the nature of God and his will for us than is revealed to us directly by the presence of God within us.

What then is included in this revelation? We perceive within us a will that seeks equally the good of all. We perceive that this will has rightful authority over all the rest of human will, so that we ought to obey it whether we want to or not. We see that it is a will, first to use human intelligence to *find* what is the greatest good for all concerned, and then to use human effort to *do* that which will produce that greatest good. We learn from others that they too have the experience within them of a will other and higher than their own private individuality. We call it God and know that God is personal, loving and righteous, the ultimate source of the moral law which requires of each that he should love God and love his neighbor, even though that neighbor should make himself an enemy.

Nothing more of the nature and will of God can we know with the certainty of divine revelation. But this is all the certainty we need for the guidance of the religious and moral life. The rest requires only that we use our intelligence to find the truth which will direct our efforts to produce the greatest good. These are problems of everyday fact, of philosophy, science, history and the understanding of human beings.

CRITERIA OF RELIGIOUS INFERENCE

The rest of our religious knowledge, therefore, is inference from our religious experience, interpreted in the light of our practical and scientific knowledge, and tested for its consistency with that which is revealed of God within us. It includes knowledge of the means of spiritual culture, of modes of worship and of religious work. This knowledge of what is good and helpful in the spiritual life of man has been accumulated in the course of history and tested in practical experience of the religious life. It includes also ideas about God that go beyond what is directly revealed within — his unity, transcendence and power, his creative activity, his relation to man and his plan for human destiny. So long as these are consistent with the revelation of God within, and with scientific and historical fact, they are possible. Some knowledge of this sort is implied with a high degree of assurance (as we have already seen) when we put together our assured religious knowledge and our well tested scientific and historical knowledge.

Still further, our religious knowledge includes inferences about the significance and importance of certain historical persons and institutions and the products of their activity, such as Christ and the prophets and apostles, the church and the Bible. We can form judgments about the relation of these to God — judgments based on observation of the function of these persons and things in what we know to fulfill the will of God. Here the criterion is, first, the consistency of these judgments with the rest of our religious, scientific and historical knowledge. Second, the criterion is practical. " By their fruits ye shall know them." How well do these judgments work in fulfilling the will of God? If a statement about Christ, or the church, or the Bible, or other religious matter, is consistent with all our knowledge, scientific, historical and religious alike, but is not implied by this knowledge, that leaves its truth an open possibility. It is, thus far, probable but neither proved nor disproved. But if, further, it can be shown that to believe this statement is morally wholesome, gives courage and strength, makes a personality glow with love and happiness, and has no harmful consequences, then that statement should rightly be accepted as a matter of *faith*. It can honestly and logically be made a practical, working postulate of daily life.

By such a faith a man may live; and in accord with it a group of people may organize their religious life into a church. But it is very plain to see that in such matters of faith all should be open-minded, undogmatic and tolerant. It does not follow that all people will find the same beliefs equally inspiring and wholesome. Where they do not a man should always remember that it may be he, not the other person, who is mistaken. The very fact that some do not find the belief convincing and wholesome suggests that it may be only partially true. At least it calls for a good explanation of the other person's error. Further, there is a positive reason for tolerance. Tolerance works well, while intolerance does not. The very practical criterion on which faith rests shows that open-mindedness and tolerance toward the beliefs of others are an excellent principle for the life of faith.

A faith which continues to work well for all who try it, and one which has been tested and accepted by millions of people, acquires something more than a practical justification. It must, to a very large extent, be factually true or it could not work so well over so large an area. A faith that works well must tend to maintain the integrity of personality; it must help in social adjustments; it must keep the individual life in harmony with God within. In so far as a faith is factually false it is apt to be misleading in some way. And this flaw must tend to show up in maladjustment of personalities and in a failure of religion to perform its function in maintaining the wholesome integration of society. Thus we can apply to every doctrine the practical criterion of its effects upon the course of history. If it has stimulated a vital and wholesome moral and religious life, and tended to create and maintain a freely advancing and well integrated social order, then it is probably true in fact as well as justified as a matter of faith. If it has had the reverse effect it is neither. If its effect has been mixed it needs careful re-examination. It is probably a mixture of truth and error.

THE CUMULATIVE WITNESS OF HISTORY

When we apply these criteria to the belief that there has been a revelation of God in history what do we find? At the beginning of this chapter we presented two theories of the source of religious knowledge. The first affirmed that the essential nature of God is continuously revealed within us so that we have only to shake off the blindness of selfishness and prejudice to see God as he is — to see him as a will that is in us, part of us, yet has authority over us, a will that seeks in and through us the good of all. The rest of our knowledge of God, on this view, is inference based on the experience of trying to live in harmony with the divine will, seeking the truth that will guide us in the effort to do good, and striving ever to realize the greatest good. Where the inferences concern God's relation to physical nature and historical persons they are apt to be more or less mistaken unless the thinker has accurate scientific and historical knowledge. But the most important requirement for insight into further truth is moral.

Only those who have seen God as he is immediately revealed within are competent to judge of his relation to the facts of science and history. And only by overcoming selfishness and prejudice can we see clearly and fully the nature and purpose of God as he is revealed within. "The pure in heart . . . shall see God" (Matt. 5:8). "If any man will do his will, he shall know of the doctrine, whether it be of God" (John 7:17). These texts recognize that insight into the true nature of God's revelation of himself to man depends primarily on the spiritual attitude of the seeker of truth. It is not that God withholds from any man any essential knowledge of him-

self, but only that because of our selfishness and prejudice we do not want to see. And only when this fundamental insight into the nature and purpose of God is
clear and full do we have a sound and sufficient basis for
accurate inference concerning his relation to physical nature and human history.

This being the case, some may ask whether it can ever
be possible for any person to see the real truth about
God, even though he is plainly revealed within us. For
are we not all blinded by selfishness and prejudice? How
then can any one of us claim to see the true nature of
God's will? The answer is that in acquiring this insight
we have help from history. Each generation has its character framed more or less thoroughly in accord with the
moral insights accumulated by its ancestors. Each begins the search for truth where the other ended. We today know that " God is love," that the moral law is in-
corporated in the Golden Rule, because these things
have been a part of our tradition since the time of Christ.

We have been told these things in our youth but because of our selfishness and prejudice we have found
them hard to believe. Yet when in our best moments
we have looked within and asked whether these principles really represent the will of God we have found
" the witness of the spirit." We have found something
within ourselves, higher than our own will and claim-
ing authority over it, demanding of us that we observe
these principles. In our selfishness and prejudice we
have been false to them, but in subsequent reflection,
when passion has died, we have seen clearly that such action is wrong. Thus we have discovered the true nature
of God within, in spite of our moral imperfection. But
we have been able to overcome the handicap only be-

cause we have been helped by others, because we are heirs to a tradition, and members of a community, in which the true nature and purpose of God were discovered long ago. Only occasionally does some great soul so overcome his selfishness and prejudice as to see God a little more clearly than any who have gone before. These are the prophets and teachers by whom the tradition has been corrected and advanced until it culminated in Christ.

It is this tradition, maintained in the life of the religious community, that preserves the revelation of God in history. It embodies a story of human religious activities and a collection of ideas that interpret the experience of God within and his relation to physical nature and historical persons. Not all these ideas are true in fact. Some of them contain partial truth. Some are clearly true. But they tell us of men's search for God and what they have believed themselves to find. Among these ideas we must sift truth from error by all the criteria of science, history and practical value, but above all by the criterion of our experience of God within.

Though this tradition inevitably contains much error, both as to historical fact and as to religious interpretation, it nevertheless is rightly recognized as also containing a revelation of God. For God is at work in man. He makes himself felt in human experience. Where there is spiritual struggle against difficulty, where critical moral decisions have to be made, there is the divine influence peculiarly felt. These are the occasions when men come face to face with God within themselves — with God in the form of the other and higher will that demands of us that we concern ourselves with the good of others. From such encounters with God lessons are learned by thoughtful, earnest and sensitive souls. New insights are obtained. New truths are grasped. Elements of falsity in past tradition are exposed and rejected. Thus the tradition is a growing and self-critical movement. It is a record of man's experience with God, always imperfectly understood, but gradually growing clearer, fuller and more accurate in its understanding of the divine will.

Within ourselves we discern God directly, but through the veil of our selfishness and prejudice. So far as his relations to the rest of the world are concerned, we see those relations from our own limited point of view. In the lives and teaching of others we can discern God indirectly, but more objectively, less affected by our own special selfishness, prejudices and point of view. The external and indirect revelation in history stimulates our perception of the revelation within and gives it concrete illustration. The revelation within checks, illuminates and confirms the revelation in history. We need both. We need to feed our minds upon the experience and thought of Christ, the apostles and prophets, and of all the great religious figures of history. For we need their stimulus and suggestion. And we need to give time for communion with God as we find him within.

THE BEGINNINGS OF RELIGION

It has been a very slow process by which man has discovered the true nature of God and his own relationship to him. Yet it has not been as slow as that by which man has learned to understand the physical world, for it reached its culmination nineteen centuries ago in the life and thought of Jesus Christ. Since then the problem has been, not that of finding the essential nature and will of God, but that of relating our knowledge of God to the rest of our knowledge, and of overcoming the self-ishness and prejudice of successive generations, which blind them and us to the truth revealed in Christ.

The process of discovery was begun by primitive man, probably by our very first human ancestors. When we understand the conditions of the knowledge of God and the conditions of life of those first human beings we can see how it must have been. Among our prehuman ancestors the group was held together instinctively by the natural impulses of its members. No animal can think for itself. Each follows its instincts. Our prehuman ancestors instinctively clung to the herd and cooperated with it in hunting and fighting. But the dawn of human intelligence made it possible for individuals to think for themselves and of themselves. Each must have begun to desire most strongly his own comfort and security. Instinctive cooperation would tend to be broken down by cunning selfishness. This must have created the first type of moral problem that human beings had to face — the temptation of individuals to shirk discomfort, fatigue and danger in the tasks they had to share in the common interest.

Thus the selfishness made possible by the new intelligence must have threatened to disrupt the first really human society. But religion came to its rescue to become the cement that bound it together. The more thoughtful and sensitive members of the primitive group must have reflected on this tendency to selfish shirking in themselves and others. They must have seen its evil effects and felt it as vaguely wrong — contrary to the peculiar authority they would feel attached to the will to the greater and common good. They would feel the constraint of the sense of guilt without being able to give it a name. On a subsequent occasion they would re-solve to bear their full share of the burden with the tribe. They would express admiration for those that did. This would be echoed by those around, and a tradition of honor would be established.

But the moral tradition would not be easy to main-tain. So, on the eve of arduous and dangerous tasks in which all the men of the tribe must join, they would meet together to plan and to give each other mutual support by expressing their intention to be true to the tribe and to quit themselves like men. Within each man there would be the battle between the individual self on the one side and, on the other, that will to the good of all which we have learned to recognize as God in us. This will to the greatest good would support the ideal of the common good of the group; and it would itself be supported by the group's authority and prestige. The constraining power of the divine will, with its sense of authority and obligation, would thus be strongly felt, being reinforced by the knowledge that its demands were supported by the tribe.   56623

Spontaneous expressions of courage and loyalty would be made and cheered. In course of time these would tend to take dramatic and ceremonial form. Dance, drama, gesture, music and shouting would heighten the effect, exerting a psychological power that was mysteri-ous and strong. This would be connected in their thought with the inner moral constraint in response to which the more dramatic ceremonies had originated. Thus the mysterious power of the ceremony would come to be identified in their thought with the power that gave the moral law. Just such a power, mystical, moral, but impersonal, is believed by all primitive people to reside in their ceremonies. Anthropologists, using the Polynesian name for it, call it "mana." This seems to be the first clearly formed religious idea. It is an interpretation of man's earliest experience of the constraining presence of God within him. And the interpretation is made in the light of his further experience of the sort of ceremonial activity that enabled him to bring himself into harmony with that higher constraining will.

From the beginning, therefore, the practices of religion became a force to bind the group together, constraining and encouraging each member to perform his recognized duties, and helping individuals to maintain their inner personal integration and moral self-respect. And the first religious idea was a mixture of truth and error. But this idea soon blossomed into others, with some new truth but more error. The mysterious moral power was naturally believed to reside in the objects used in the ceremonies, e.g., the totem pole or earlier tribal insignia, the grove where the ceremony was performed, the dress and properties for dramatic parts. The animal badge of the tribe, or totem, being regarded as the chief seat of the mysterious moral power, was personalized and became an animal god. All the mysteries of nature came to be interpreted as due to this same mysterious power. Thus arose nature deities, some good, some bad. Men persuaded themselves that mysterious dramatic rites could control the mysterious power in their own interests. Thus magic came into religion and obscured its moral significance.

THE PROGRESS OF RELIGION

As civilization developed some individuals secured leisure for reflection and began to criticize, develop and refine their religious ideas. Very early in Egyptian civilization there arose a priesthood which secured its leisure by its special skill in the practice of religious ceremonies and used this leisure to ponder the problems of life, both religious and practical. The priesthood contributed a great deal to Egyptian knowledge before the year 4000 B.C. It developed land surveying, irrigation, methods of calculation, writing, law, and a lofty type of religious thought in which one personal deity was thought to be supreme above all gods and men, and the source of the moral law. It insisted that even the king must obey the moral law and developed the belief in a future life in which men would be rewarded according to their deeds. Unfortunately the priests also developed a great deal of magic as a means of avoiding dangers in this life and averting punishment in the next, and this eventually undermined the good effect of the rest of their religion.

From the Egyptians the leadership in the development of religious thought passed to the Hebrews. It is impossible, with our present historical knowledge, to decide how much of the stories of Abraham, Moses and other figures in the early Old Testament record is historical. But it is evident that, when the Hebrews conquered Palestine, they had a good many rather primitive religious ideas akin to those of other Semitic tribes of the desert; but they also had some very special and definitely higher ideas connected with the god Yahweh (Jehovah) which they asserted had been taught them by Moses.

The content of this teaching bears out the claim that Moses was " learned in all the wisdom of the Egyptians." Yet it indicates, too, that he was a prophet and thinker in his own right, for the teaching (if it can indeed be attributed to him) repudiates idolatry and the cult of the dead and other magical features that disfigured and undermined the religious life of Egypt.

We reach sound historical ground in the writings of the Hebrew prophets from the eighth to the end of the sixth century B.C. And a magnificent advance in moral and religious ideas they achieve. They teach that there is one supreme deity whose will is eternally righteous and good. He rules sternly, but he loves his children as a father. It is his will that every man should love his neighbor (meaning his own people) as himself. Even to a stranger he should do no injustice. The existing injustices of the Hebrew social system the prophets roundly condemned. The earlier of these prophets even attempted to repudiate the blood sacrifices, with their magical notions of atonement, that the Hebrews had inherited from their Semitic antecedents. But in this they were unsuccessful, on account of priestly opposition, and the later prophets accepted the limitation of the sacrifices to the temple at Jerusalem.

Finally, we come to the consummation of this development in the teaching of Christ. All the limits to the law of love are at last abolished. " Love your neighbor " means even " Love your enemy." Jew and Gentile, master and slave, male and female, all share equally in God's love and concern and must share equally in ours. Death can be faced in confidence of God's eternal love for all his children. To the law of love we must be faithful even unto death — and even unto the death of the cross.

THE UNIVERSALITY OF REVELATION

The whole history of religion, with all its human error, passion and frailty, is the story of man's search for God. And those who seek him find him. And those who find him help others to find him. God is found by man because he is actively revealed to man. Not just on special occasions, to selected individuals of selected groups or tribes, in dark and mysterious ways or in dramatic and miraculous form. But *always,* at every waking hour, in every human mind, God is present and his will is *fully* revealed. It is because God is at work in every man, and revealed to every man, that God is at work in history.

But most of us are more or less blinded by our habits and natural impulses, our selfishness, passion, pride and prejudice. We are slow to see, slow to understand, slow to admit the truth. That is why there is a *special* revelation of God in history. It could not be otherwise. For some individuals have sought God with purer hearts and more open minds than others, as well as with greater earnestness and intelligence. These have come to see God's will more clearly than their fellows and have recognized its meaning for their own lives and their own times. They have thus become teachers of new truth about God, prophets with a new insight into his will, writers inspired by the direct vision of God more clearly discerned than by those around them.

The record of this special revelation contains much error, both historical and religious. Yet there is a clearly defined line of advance running through it all. It runs from narrow interest in the welfare of a special group to universal interest in the welfare of all mankind; from reliance upon external forms to emphasis on the inward spirit of whole-souled devotion; from a few specific moral injunctions to the free and intelligent pursuit of the greatest good of all; from the mysticism of mere magic to that of inner communion with the divine; from a multiplicity of divine beings confined to special times, places and functions to one God who is in all and over all.

This line of advance, more or less complete, is found not only in the Hebrew-Christian tradition but, still earlier, in ancient Egypt and Mesopotamia, and independently developing in Greece, Persia, India and China. The specific history, and the errors and evils, differ from one place to another. But in each there is the same progressive discovery of religious truth. From the time of the great prophets of the eighth century B.C., if not from Moses or Abraham, the Hebrews are ahead of the rest of the world; and they first attain the full vision, positive, unqualified and unambiguous, in the life and teaching of Christ. But the others are never far behind and their loftiest vision does not fall far short. God is as surely present in the one as the other, inspiring the prophets and revealing himself to the saints of all the world.

Today all the great streams of this process of divine revelation and human insight have come to knowledge of each other. The non-Christian religions are reinterpreting, purifying and enriching their tradition in the light of the Christian vision. The Christian is checking its errors, especially the error of its imagined exclusive possession of a genuine revelation, by what it learns of the mighty working of God in histories other than its own.

This is the Christian doctrine of revelation, reinterpreted in the light of our modern knowledge of natural science, history and psychology, and tested by its consistency with our inner vision of God as illuminated by the life and teaching of Christ. Does it also stand the practical test of value for the spiritual life?

Briefly and emphatically the answer is " Yes." It gives us an authority for the supreme law of love to all mankind — an authority that is above all human law and all individual desires. It therefore answers man's great need, for fulfillment of which he can look to no other source but religion: it gives him an authoritative principle for the unifying of the individual life and the maintenance of a social order concerned equally with the good of all. At the same time it frees us from all specific dogmatism and from the demand of any institutions for unquestioning obedience, for we must seek with all our intelligence the means to the good of all. It sets the scholar free to carry on his investigations in science and history, untrammeled by any dogma. It abolishes all religious exclusiveness, enabling us to welcome light from every source, to recognize the working of God in the history of every religion and every society, and therefore to give the full measure of respect to God's children everywhere. It points us clearly to the central figure of Christ as the consummation of the special revelation of God in history, and enables us to understand, appreciate and cherish that Christian heritage which has meant so much to the world. Finally, it shows that, in nearly every religious tradition, God has led men to the conviction that his eternal love cares, not only for their earthly lives and service, but also for their immortal souls.

FALSE CONCEPTIONS OF REVELATION

In most of the great religious traditions, however, we find a belief in a more specific historical revelation than

is here recognized. It is claimed that the eternal consciousness imparts a special communication of ideas to
selected persons, verbally or otherwise. These are recorded in sacred books. Their divine origin is believed
to be attested by special signs, such as miracles, visions,
voices or some strangely convincing inner experience.

The chief difficulty with this belief is the amount of
error and contradiction in the messages said to have been
received and endorsed in this way. Mohammedan, Bud-
dhist, Hindu, Zoroastrian, Jewish and Christian scriptures all claim that their mutually contradictory doctrines have been thus established. When it is recognized
that this cannot be the case it is natural to claim the truth
for one's own doctrines and reject the others. This leads
to religious arrogance and intolerance; it denies the reality of God's relation to man outside the circle of one religion. It claims the truth, the whole truth and nothing
but the truth for one body of scriptures. But it cannot
substantiate this claim.

Even the Hebrew-Christian scriptures are not free
from contradiction. For example, it is recorded (Exod.
26:9–11) that Moses and Aaron, with seventy of the
elders of Israel, went up on Mount Sinai and " they saw
the God of Israel "; yet, with the New Testament's more
spiritual conception of deity, we are told (John 1:18)
that " no man hath seen God at any time." Again, in
connection with the giving of the Ten Commandments,
God is presented as endorsing the primitive principle of
collective responsibility: " I the Lord thy God am a jeal-
ous God, visiting the iniquity of the fathers upon the
children to the third and fourth generation of them that
hate me " (Exod. 20:5) . But later prophets repudiate

this barbarism, preaching individual responsibility: "The soul that sinneth, it shall die. The son shall not bear the iniquity of the father, neither shall the father bear the iniquity of the son" (Ezek. 18:20). This is but one illustration of the great moral advance from the earlier to the later parts of the Hebrew-Christian scriptures. To give just one more example we may point to the law of retribution in Exodus 21:23–24: "Thou shalt give life for life, eye for eye, tooth for tooth." With this we may compare the Sermon on the Mount: "Love your enemies, bless them that persecute you, do good to them that hate you, and pray for them that despitefully use you and persecute you" (Matt. 5:44).

If the revelation of God in history were given as a communication of ideas then the eternal consciousness must be accused of first putting wrong ideas into men's minds and later contradicting them. It is not merely a matter of adapting instruction to the level of the minds to receive it, but of giving false instruction. The notions of a visible deity, collective responsibility and the justification of revenge are false ideas and could not have been communicated to men by the eternal consciousness. They are the result of man's imperfect vision of God, seen through the veil of selfishness, passion and prejudice, and distorted in interpretations affected by scientific and historical ignorance.

The claims to endorsement of this type of revelation by miracle, vision and mystic experience carry no weight. Modern psychological investigation of perfectly honest human testimony has shown that eyewitness reports are constantly in error. Rumors can grow and acquire wide belief in a few hours. Visions and mystical experiences of a sensory and emotional character have a natural psychological explanation. " Miracles " of healing are likewise explained by abnormal psychology. Great religious teachers, living in an age of superstition, inevitably generate an expectation of wonders; and the expectation produces some wonders by the force of suggestion and adds to the report of these by its power to propagate rumors.

Great religious teachers, furthermore, are usually people who have won their new religious insights only after severe spiritual trial and brave conflict with the passions of their own souls and those of others. It is not surprising, therefore, that the insights thus gained are frequently accompanied by the feeling of a heart that is " strangely warmed," the attainment of a wonderful sense of peace and blessedness, and even the seeing of visions and the hearing of voices. These are natural accompaniments of spiritual struggle and triumph. And it is only by spiritual struggle that men triumph over the factors which render them blind to the true nature of the will of God within.

The same objection applies to the claim that the " witness of the spirit " affects individuals in spiritual crises so that they discern the true meaning for themselves of the revelation contained in scriptures. This claim is sound only so far as it refers to a recognition of the harmony of some scriptural teaching with the will of God as found within. If the endorsement of the " inner witness " is alleged to consist of strange feelings of conviction, of enlightenment, of joy and enthusiasm, of assurance, or of visions or voices, it must be recognized as simply a natural psychological effect of the emotional tensions involved in the spiritual crisis. Experiences of this sort may accompany a genuine insight into the will of God. But they do nothing to enhance the assurance of its accuracy.

The real test of all insights is their harmony with what the long history of man's moral and religious development, culminating in Christ, has shown to be the will of God — that we should love one another as Christ has loved us. This growing agreement and wonderful culmination is the real meaning of the revelation of God in history.

THE LIMITATION AND SUFFICIENCY OF REVELATION

One further argument for a specific communication of ideas from God to man is that there must be some such revelation because there *ought* to be. If God loves his children, it is pointed out, then he would wish to communicate with them; and since they need the truths he can give them, then it would not be right that he should neglect to teach them. We may agree that God must be willing to teach us all that he can, so far as it is to our good. But there is much that would be to our good that he has certainly let us slowly discover for ourselves. Has God, though able to give man the knowledge, let him suffer for ages from his ignorance of how to live a healthy physical life and how to organize a free and stable social order? There is no moral value in ignorance. There would be no moral loss in learning these things completely and accurately from a God-given Bible instead of incompletely and never quite accurately from human textbooks.

Since God ought to reveal these things if he can, and yet has not revealed them, the only conclusion is that he cannot do so. And if he cannot communicate specific ideas concerning a sound health program, neither can he

be expected to communicate specific ideas concerning
civil law or church organization. So we must ask the reason of such limitation to God's power.

The answer seems clearly to be in the nature of the
finite human mind. Ideas, or meanings, are developed
by the activity of a specific type of mental organization.
Only a mind with a similar type of organization could
hold similar ideas. So only similar types of mind can
communicate ideas to each other. Our type of mental
organization is developed through physical life on earth.
So we can expect to have intercommunication of ideas
only with other finite personalities developed on earth.
God is aware of the ideas in our minds because our minds
are a part of his. Each finite mind is a relatively independent interest-process within the universal mind. But
the finite mind is not aware of other interests and ideas
in the eternal consciousness which is the ultimate source
of its life. Nor can these ideas of the eternal consciousness be communicated to finite minds, on account of the
different and highly specialized organization of finite
minds and their limited means of comprehension. The
influence of God's mind upon us is through his will
which is ever present in us. We cannot arbitrarily say
that it can have no influence upon us in any other way.
But it certainly does not seem to include the possibility
of any direct communication of ideas from the eternal
consciousness to ours.

We must be content, therefore, with the revelation of
God's will as it operates within, helped by what we learn
from others through the operation of God's will in them.
This gives us sufficient assurance for our moral and religious life. And if we look to it alone we shall be saved
from the errors into which men have constantly strayed

through seeking more specific revelations of God elsewhere. It is the claim, by individuals and groups, that they have specific revelations concerning the moral and civil law, and concerning the doctrine, worship and organization of the church, that is the chief source of the sectarianism, intolerance, dogmatism and strife which have disgraced the history of Christianity and other religions. Judged by the criterion of its practical effects the doctrine of a revelation in the form of specific ideas or dogmas is condemned one hundredfold. Because of its contradictions and falsities it is condemned, too, by science and history. Religion must shake itself free from this doctrine and its accompanying magic. When it does that, and learns to rely primarily upon the inner witness of the spirit to the eternal validity of the Golden Rule, it will function as it should, as the inspiration to all that is best in life, the buttress of the social order, the support of human liberty, and the saver of souls.

Is Christianity the Final Religion?

CHRIST'S PLACE IN WORLD RELIGION

GOD IS in all men, Christian and non-Christian, and thereby his will is revealed to all who open their eyes to see. Prophets have arisen among all peoples, and truly great prophets in Egypt, India, China, Persia, Greece and Arabia as well as in Palestine. The knowledge of God has grown, in all these countries, from primitive beginnings to lofty spiritual insight. Prophets and teachers in each of the great traditions have learned something from outside their own tradition, and continue to do so. The revelation of God in history has not ceased but is active in all men at all times. The significance of that revelation for special problems of our own day is seen with fresh insight, more or less clear and full, by leaders in every religious tradition still current. None can afford to ignore the insights and teaching of others. None should deny the operation of the divine will in influencing the thoughts of others. None can claim for his own thought the whole truth and nothing but the truth. Every teacher should be a learner with an open mind and a heart humble enough to receive truth from every quarter.

What becomes then of the claim to finality for the Christian religion? What justification is there for the missionary effort to convert the world to Christ? Is it possible that Christ may some day be transcended by a still greater religious teacher?

In answer to these questions it may be definitely stated that, in the most important matter of all, Christianity is final and the place of Christ in God's revelation in history is unique.   In Christ we find the culmination of the historic revelation of God's will, as a will to the good of all, to be pursued without exception and without limit. It is true that essentially the same idea finds occasional expression among Stoic philosophers, Jewish rabbis and Oriental sages.   Since God is in us, striving to direct our minds to this goal, it would be strange if no glimmering of it were found elsewhere.   But no teacher before Christ made it the essential, central and dominant theme of his moral teaching, as Jesus did.   No other thinker carried it so clearly to its logical conclusion: " Love your enemies."   No other teacher maintained it so consistently in every phase of his discourse, or exemplified it so thoroughly in his life and death.   No other leader succeeded in establishing a great religious movement, permeated with the spirit of this ideal and dedicated to its propagation throughout the world.

Because Jesus did these things his position is unique in history.   No conception of human duty can be greater or truer than that which demands from each the utmost effort to pursue disinterestedly the good of all.   No life can be nobler than one which is daily consecrated to that end and gives to it at length the last full measure of devotion.   The best of those who come after him can do no more than follow in his train.   Neither the ideal itself, nor the measure of devotion to it, can they ever exceed. And those who follow after cannot, and do not, claim equality with the leader who blazed the trail.   The best of them are clearest in their acknowledgment that without his guidance they could not have seen the way and with-

out the inspiration of his example their hearts would
often fail. Every age presents new problems, and offers
new light on the means to deal with the old. The problems change, new victories are won, and the methods improve, but the end remains the same. It is the goal that
is set before all men by the will of God within, and its
nature has been clarified, once and for all, by the life and
teaching of Jesus Christ.

Because of what Christ has done for the world the
world should know, not only of his teaching, but of him.
It is not charity to withhold that teaching from non-
Christian peoples. It is not humility to give the teaching
without acknowledging the teacher whence we received
it. The Christian is not true to his own ideal if he fails
to be a missionary in every way he can. But he is not
true to his ideal, either, if he performs his mission in a
spirit of arrogance and pride. Many have made that mistake. And it has naturally aroused the pride of the non-
Christian to resist the new teaching. But the remedy is
not to give up the missionary effort, but to perform it in
a spirit of humility and love which is alive to all the truth
and value in the non-Christian religions. Thus presented Christianity may be more readily received as a
fulfillment, purification and consummation of that vision of God which each religion cherishes as its own.

THE DIVINITY OF CHRIST

Because of Christ's place in history we can rightly say
that we see in him the full and final revelation of God
to man. Because his personal life so completely expressed the will of God we can agree with the writer of
the Fourth Gospel that in him " the Word became flesh
and dwelt among us " (John 1:14). The eternal will

of God, creatively active in the development of life on earth, produced at last in him a complete expression of its own true nature as the will to universal good.

Further, we can speak of him as " the Son of God." God is the source of all life. We are not created things external to his being, but offspring of the divine life. It is more fact than metaphor to speak of God as our Father and of all men as his children. It is therefore perfectly legitimate to speak of Jesus Christ, whose life expressed in its fullness the will of God in finite human form, as *the* Son of God, pre-eminent among all men as an expression of the divine nature.

Here we see the solution of the controversy about the divinity of Christ that has plagued Christian theology for so many centuries. Jesus combined true humanity and true divinity in the only way they could be combined. He was a real person, distinct from the real personality of the eternal consciousness. Yet his personality (like all living things) had its root and source in the eternal consciousness and was (and is) inseparable from it. And (unlike other living things) his personality expressed to the full the essential nature of the eternal consciousness as a will to the good of all. Yet it was at the same time limited in knowledge and power in the same way as other human personalities.

It was by a sound prophetic insight that the early disciples of Christ declared him both fully human and fully divine, though they had no philosophy whereby to explain it. When, a little later, they sought to interpret their faith in terms of Greek philosophy they found themselves enmeshed in difficulties; but they clung to their religious insight. In the course of Christian history the doctrine has proved its value in giving vitality to the

Christian faith.   Those sects that have denied it in the effort to make their theology more rational have found their religion devitalized and their numbers and influence have diminished.   The recognition that Jesus is the Son of God gives concrete reality and warmth to the abstract statement that " God is love."

Something, however, must be said for those who have rejected the doctrine of Christ's divinity in the name of reason.   The failure of theology to do justice to the presence of God in man as the will to the greatest good made it impossible to work out a reasonable understanding of the relation of God and man.   It set God off too far from man.   And to call Christ divine therefore set him off too far from man.   It made his personality something miraculous and encouraged superstition.   It led to the conception of the Christian religion as so distinct from other religions that it filled all too many Christians with a spirit of arrogance and pride.   This situation will continue until Christian theology can rectify its fundamental error — the failure to recognize fully and clearly the presence of God in every man.

The view that is here presented makes the life and example of Christ no less divine.   But it enables us to see more clearly the divine agency also in other religions than our own.   And it enables us to contemplate the divinity of Christ without losing the full appreciation of his humanity in feelings of mystification and awe, and without relying on dubious stories of his miraculous birth which would make him only half human and half divine.

Unitarians and atheists err in saying that Jesus was a " mere man."   But the root of their error is shared by many " orthodox " persons in assuming that there can be any such creature as a *mere* man.   There is not.   God is in all of us.   Without the divine will as the foundation of personality human individuality could not exist. But the divine in most of us is largely hidden by the human individuality, our private, individual habits of will running counter to the divine.   In Jesus the divine will not merely shines through the human, but is revealed in it; his human, individual will is a direct expression of the divine.   God is, in him, manifest in the flesh.   The divine is seen expressing itself in a human life, from a finite, limited, human point of view.

Even the apostle Paul, who clearly teaches that " it is God which worketh in us to will and to do of his good pleasure," was not able to grasp the intimacy of the relation between man and God.   Only the modern understanding of personality as an organization of will, which can be organically interconnected with higher and lower organizations of will (higher and lower persons) , makes this possible.   Before this was explained by modern psychological investigation, personality was generally thought to belong to a unique unit of soul-substance. Therefore, if Jesus was divine, his personality had to be thought of as belonging to an eternal soul-substance. Paul thus thought of him as eternally existing " in the form of God " and voluntarily blotting out his divine consciousness to take on " the likeness of men " (Phil. 2:5–8) .   This presents an appealing picture of high self-sacrifice which many are loath to surrender.   But the self-sacrifice of a divine being, who undertakes a temporary and painful mission of tremendous importance, is really on a much lower plane than that of " the man Christ Jesus," who must walk by faith and not by sight. There is nothing really lost when we give up the Pauline

picture.   On the contrary, Jesus is brought much closer
to us in both his divinity and his humanity.

THE CHRISTIAN IDEA OF SALVATION

Thus far we have considered the claim to finality of the
Christian religion as resting on the completeness of the
Christian ethic, the place of Jesus in history, and the divinity of his nature.   But the claim to finality rests still
more emphatically on the significance of Christianity as
a way of salvation, both for the individual and for society.

It is certainly a misrepresentation of Christian teaching to say that there is no salvation outside of Christianity.   The Epistle to the Hebrews (chap. 11) tells of many
Old Testament heroes (not all Hebrews) who were saved
by faith without the knowledge of Christ.   And the apostle Paul says that the Gentiles are judged of God, not
by Hebrew or Christian standards, but by the law endorsed by their own consciences (Rom. 2:13–15).   So
when Peter in his enthusiasm exclaims, " For there is
none other name under heaven given among men
whereby we must be saved " (Acts 4:12), his statement
must be qualified by reference to these other texts.   Yet
Christianity certainly has claimed, in relation to Christ,
a unique divine provision for salvation from sin.   In so
far as it has suggested that there is no salvation for anyone except by believing in Christian doctrine the claim
must be rejected as injurious and false.   But in so far as
it asserts that faith in Christ gives to man a unique aid
in his struggle with sin it is abundantly verified in religious experience.

The Christian claim to finality as a way of salvation
should therefore be interpreted as recognizing that salvation means the overcoming of the effects of sin upon the

human soul, both for this life and for eternity. And this is, plainly, a matter of degrees. The claim of Christianity to finality as a way of salvation is therefore simply a claim to completeness. Christ is able to save " to the uttermost " those who put their trust in him, who follow his way. And nothing less than the Christian way can lead to complete salvation. This is the claim which we must investigate. We must inquire into the nature of sin in its effects upon the human soul and see how salvation from these is wrought by faith in Christ.

SIN AND MORAL FREEDOM

Sin is not necessarily the same thing as doing wrong or producing evil. A child may do wrong in complete ignorance and innocence. Even an animal or a storm can produce evil, but they cannot sin. To say that an act is sinful is to imply that the person who did it is morally to be blamed for it. This means that he could have avoided committing the wrong or producing the evil, or that he could have produced a greater good. It means that he could have done something better if only he had made the necessary effort. There are sins of omission as well of commission. Sin is a *failure* to produce the greater good or the lesser evil when, by some action of ours, a greater good or lesser evil was possible. It implies that we were free to avoid the evil action or to do something better and yet failed to exercise this freedom. Only in so far as we are free agents is it possible to be guilty of sin.

There are many kinds of freedom, but they all involve one essential condition. The free agent has some power of *self-determination*. It is not entirely controlled by external conditions. Men and animals have a certain

physical freedom, but it is strictly limited by external
physical conditions. They also have a certain social freedom, limited by the compulsions imposed by other individuals. Within these limits men and animals are both
free. And they produce both good and evil. But man
has a further freedom which the animal has not. The
animal is a slave to his inherited natural impulses and
fixed habits. Man can choose between different goods
and evils in a way that the animal cannot. We must examine this difference carefully.

Even the animal has some power of choice. Between
two foods he chooses the one he likes better. Between
his desire for food and his fear of a whip he chooses the
alternative that impresses him less painfully. But in
these choices he is still a slave to impulses and habits. He
is carried away by the drive that is strongest at the moment. And the strength of that drive is determined by
forces beyond his present control. Many of man's choices
are on the same level. He can see further ahead than the
animal and can see a wider range of distinct possibilities
of good and evil. But often he merely responds to which-
ever of these possibilities makes the strongest appeal to
him. And the strength of their various appeals depends
upon his natural impulses and his acquired habitual
tendencies. At this level of choice man, like the animal,
is free to choose what he wants. But *what* he wants is
determined by forces beyond his present control. He
is still a slave to his own specific natural impulses and
habits.

Each one of these impulses and habits is a specific,
fixed form of will. It is a tendency to strive for some
specific good. Some of these specific drives have been
developed in the history of the race and are inherited in

our animal nature, like the drives to satisfy hunger and sex and to escape from pain. Some of these inherited drives have become highly specialized in particular habits, and other habits have been developed that cannot easily be traced to any one particular animal drive. Each of them begins as a response to some particular feeling or anticipation of satisfaction or dissatisfaction. Thus they are all, at first, purely egoistic. They aim at something felt as good, but only at private, personal satisfactions. The infant is unaware of any good but his own and the habits formed in infancy are therefore purely selfish.

These infantile tendencies are modified somewhat, and an important additional set of habits is developed, by social training. Each social group to which the individual belongs — the family, the local community, the nation, the school, etc. — has its own special set of interests, and trains the individual to serve those interests. This training modifies selfishness but creates new evils. For the interests of one group are often antagonistic to those of another and the individual is trained to hate, fear and despise, as well as to love, admire and obey. And nearly always the group trains the individual to put the interests of his own group before those of other groups. Thus arise the narrow loyalties that tear human society into conflicting groups.

Every specific tendency of will, whether inherited or acquired, is an impulsion to seek some good. But because these specific tendencies, which constitute our individuality, are narrow and limited in their aims they drive us again and again to destroy the greater good or produce some balance of evil in our pursuit of the lesser goods toward which they impel us. When we do this in spite of an awareness of the balance of evil, or loss of greater good, it is sin.

Thus sin often has the appearance of a positive effort to produce evil, because goods are destroyed and positive evils produced in the effort to produce a lesser good. Yet there is no such thing as a will to evil for its own sake. Anger is an impulse to destroy that which creates fear or impedes satisfaction of some desire. Hatred is an attitude of mind developed by such strong and frequent anger that the hater identifies any evil to the person hated with a good to himself. Thus the evil and the tragedy grow out of our limitations, our finitude, not out of the essential nature and aim of human will.

It is a mistake to think that there must be some demonic tendency, some positive love of evil in man, to explain the horrors of human cruelty. Perverted minds, abnormally twisted, obtain a gratifying sense of power and other devious satisfactions from inflicting pain on others. The selfish drives of the infantile ego have a long start over the altruistic tendencies in the development of the child. And the narrow family and tribal loyalties have a long start in the history of the race. The wonder is, not that man is so careless of the good of others, but that these selfish and narrow impulses can ever be overcome. If the will to the good of others were just another one of the many specific forms of will, developed in the history of the race and the individual, it never could triumph over the others as it does.

How does this will to the greater good exert any control over the established forces of the narrow special interests? It is here that we approach the question of the operation of man's higher freedom. The need and the opportunity for its exercise arise when there is conflict within the personality. For example, specific habits and impulses direct a man's attention to a goal wherein is found the satisfaction of some special interest. It is *his* good or the good of *his* group. But there is another possibility of a greater good of some other person at stake. The situation is such that he must choose between them. The will to the *greatest* good makes itself felt, but it lacks the drive and the emotional force of the personal or group interest; though perhaps it is supported by some specific interests, such as self-respect. There is tension and conflict within the self. The personal or group interest has the stronger driving force, but the idea of the greater good has attached to it that peculiar constraining influence which we call the sense of obligation. In response to this the self, torn by conflicting purposes, makes a unique effort. It pulls itself together, integrates itself, by subjecting the special habitual impulses to the prior claim of the will to the greatest good, as indicated by the sense of obligation.

Because the self, when threatened with disintegration, has this unique power of reintegrating itself by special effort of will it is able to maintain some degree of freedom from the enslaving power of specialized natural impulses and habits. It can pursue what appears to it as the greatest good for itself or others, even against the strong drive of long established habits and deep-rooted natural impulses. Its freedom is limited. It may find impulse and habit sometimes too strong for it. But it is often aided by other specific impulses, especially self-respect and special affections for family and friends. Thus gradually it can modify the personality and build a character which, in general, comforms to the will to the greatest good.

SIN AS SPIRITUAL INERTIA

The will to the greatest good is God within us, making his presence and authority known in the sense of obligation. Our specific impulses and habits (or specific interests) are our own individuality. When the self pulls itself together, reintegrates itself, it reintegrates its specific individuality in harmony with the divine within. It is the surrender of the private, finite self to God. But it is at the same time man's assertion of his own highest freedom, whereby he makes himself at one with God. To fail thus to assert our moral freedom is sin. Sin is a spiritual inertia that leaves us enslaved to impulse and habit, to special interest and particular passion. We sin, not in our freedom, but in our slavery. And in sinning we cut ourselves off from God. In striving for what we see as right we assert our true freedom and enter into closer communion with the divine.

This is the secret of the challenging teaching of Jesus concerning sin. For him it is not the overt act that is sin, but the failure to quell the evil desire — the lust and the anger that, when harbored in the heart, blind us to the divine will within, put us out of touch with God. And it is not the overt act that constitutes righteousness, but rather the *striving* to do right. " Blessed are they which do hunger and thirst after righteousness " (Matt. 5:6). " Joy shall be in heaven over one sinner that repenteth, more than over ninety and nine just persons that need no repentance " (Luke 15:7). The publican, who could only beat his breast and say, " God be merciful to me a sinner," was justified rather than the Pharisee who kept the law strictly but was blind to his own faults and so never strove to do better (Luke 18).

This last example shows that there can be spiritual inertia at a high level of overt action as well as at a low. And spiritual inertia is sin. It is easy for some people to be righteous, as the world counts righteousness, for they have had everything in their favor in home environment and training. It is hard for others, who have had to fight against bad environment and special temptations. But every man can *try*. He can " hunger and thirst after righteousness." So long as he keeps on striving to do right he is spiritually alive and growing. Progress is being made and heaven rejoices over it. His conscience keeps him aware of God and his effort saves him from falling away.

But spiritual stagnation sets in when a person becomes self-righteous, content with his own goodness, blind to his own imperfection. Whether his habits are predominantly good or bad such a person is " dead in trespasses and sin." He is spiritually inert. He makes no further progress but inevitably slips backward, finding excuses for himself. He becomes blind to the higher will, the will to the greatest good, which is God within him. He pays no attention to it because he does not want to be accused by it, to be called on to make an effort to do something more for his fellows than his easy and comfortable habits lead him to do. He is out of touch with God.

The problem of overcoming sin is thus the problem of overcoming spiritual inertia, at whatever level it may be found, high or low. And this is the function of Christ in the world. For our salvation from sin we need to be made conscious of our shortcomings, not only of the avoidable wrongs we have committed but of the good we might have done and have not. Salvation from sin requires that we be constantly stirred from our tendency

to lapse into spiritual inertia. We must come under
" conviction of sin." Only thereby do we awaken to the
presence within of a will that is other and higher than our
own — the will of God. Only thus can we be moved to
strive for a closer harmony with him. Only thus is spiritual effort aroused. And without spiritual effort man is
a creature of impulse and habit, living on the training
imparted to him by others. Without spiritual effort each
generation must slip back below the moral attainment of
the last until man is demoralized, animalized, and civilization sinks into chaos. Only if spiritual effort can be
kept alive, even on the highest levels of human moral attainment, can moral progress and the progress of civilization go on.

THE OVERCOMING OF SIN

Can anyone who really knows Christ be content with
himself? Can we read the Gospel story, listen to his
teaching, walk with him from Galilee to Calvary, then
measure ourselves by his moral stature and still be smugly
self-satisfied — " just persons who need no repentance "?
However good a man is, if he will honestly compare himself with Christ it must shake him from any tendency to
spiritual inertia — which is sin, and spiritual death.
However bad a man is, and insensitive to his badness, if
he really gives attention to the life and teaching of Jesus
it can scarcely fail to impress him with a sense of his
shortcomings and stir him to some effort to raise the level
of his conduct.

It is not merely the life and teaching of Jesus that is
needed to have this effect, but also his death. The lofty
teaching, above the level of any continuous human attainment, is necessary to keep before us an ideal that

forever calls for our utmost effort. But the precept would be of little avail without the example. And the example of high courage, unquenchable loving-kindness and complete devotion could be given only under conditions of supreme trial. Without that terrible testing ordeal the manifestation of God in man would have been incomplete. Jesus did not seek a martyr's death. But he could not continue his mission and avoid it. To give up teaching and go into retirement would have been the end of the movement he had started. He chose to be true to his high calling. He endured the cross and it became the crown and completion of his mission to men. Once and for all it was made manifest that a man may walk with God, may *be divine*. And none of us can look on him and honestly deny our insufficiency. He convicts us of sin. He penetrates even that wall of spiritual pride which is the last defense of the sinning self against God. It is our part then to confess to God our sinfulness, to repent, which means to *strive* to overcome it; and in that very effort we find ourselves entering again into harmony with God.

This is the atonement, the making of man *at one* with God. It is wrought within us by the recognition and confession to God of our sinfulness and by the repentance whereby we strive to live in harmony with God. And both of these are the results of faith. Faith includes some form of belief, but its basis is a moral attitude, the product of moral judgment, decision and effort, especially effort. The essence of faith is faithfulness. Faith in God means faithfulness to God. It results in maintaining that clear recognition of our insufficiency, that awareness of the reality of God as author of the moral law within, which issue in the effort that maintains our harmony with God — our at-one-ment. And this faith in God, whereby we are made at one with him, is wrought in the Christian by the knowledge of Christ and the working of the divine will within.

This does not mean that faith and salvation from sin can be brought about in no other way save through the knowledge of Christ. We have already seen that Christianity must not, and the New Testament does not, claim any such thing. God's power and means of grace are not so limited as that. But it does mean that Christ is abundantly able to save, can save to the uttermost. And nothing less than Christ — his lofty teaching, his life, his sacrifice — can do it completely, breaking the last barriers of spiritual pride. And since Christ has done it there is no need that it should be done again; nor has any other done the same. Thus, in the work of Christ in saving men from sin Christianity is seen, once again, to be the final religion.

THEORIES OF ATONEMENT

It was very difficult for the early Christian church to understand the atoning work of Christ. They felt its power in freeing them from the fear of divine condemnation because of sin, and creating in their hearts the assurance of the divine presence. They preached it as a fact of spiritual experience. But at first they made little attempt to explain it. The difficulty lay in the traditional conception of sin. For though they recorded Christ's teaching on sin in the Gospels it was too revolutionary to be fully grasped at first. In the traditional conception, sin was the overt act of breaking the divinely given moral law; and this involved penalties. The Hebrews had long sought divine forgiveness by making special sacrifices.

The prophets from Amos to Jeremiah had protested against the idea that spilling the blood of animals could atone for the sin of a man's soul. They called for repentance as the only true way of salvation. But repentance is hard and the people continued, with the encouragement of the priests, to salve their consciences at the altars.

To those who thought about it the practice of sacrificial atonement seemed logical so long as sin was regarded as simply a breaking of certain specific laws. One could keep most of the law most of the time, and could make up for the occasional lapses by taking the trouble to perform some special act of beneficence to man, or honor and worship toward God, over and above the duties imposed by the moral law. But this comfortable theory breaks down when the moral law is conceived as demanding the utmost possible effort in the service of God and man. There can be no making up for sins of omission and commission by doing good to man or honor to God that it would, in any case, be sin to neglect — and we owe all possible good to man and honor to God. So there is no possibility of special atonement by special services to God or man.

St. Paul saw this clearly. And he knew the impossibility of any man's attaining perfection in this life. The animal impulses, egoistic habits and narrow group interests which drive us to be false to the divine will within he spoke of as " the law of sin which is in my members, warring against the law of my mind, and bringing me into captivity to the law of sin " (Rom. 7:23). Yet he felt the power of that spiritual awakening, and that more intimate awareness of the precious but awesome presence of God within, which had been wrought in his complacent Pharisaic heart by the knowledge of Christ. He

felt himself convicted of sin, yet saved from its power and
accepted by God, at one with him.   And this he rightly
attributed to the new faith in God which he had found
through Christ, with its resultant penitence and spiritual
effort.   " A man is justified by faith without the deeds of
the law " (Rom. 6:28) .

Thus Paul understood, in part at least, the meaning of
the beatitude, " Blessed are they which do hunger and
thirst after righteousness: for they shall be filled " (Matt.
5:6) . Not by the overt act of obedience to a law, which
may be easy for some and psychologically impossible for
others, do we overcome the spiritual inertia which is sin,
but by that holy discontent with our lesser selves and that
striving after the ideal which are the life of faith.   " This
is the victory that overcometh the world, even our faith "
(I John, 5:4) .

But Paul's mind was obsessed with another problem.
He rightly saw that God's problem with man is to awaken
him from the spiritual inertia into which he is apt to
fall, and that this can be done for all men by the power
of the gospel of Christ if they will but attend to it.   But
he could not help thinking of the moral law on the familiar analogy of the laws made by man.   Every law of
the state requires a penalty attached to it so that it can
be enforced.   Otherwise it is useless.   And a just ruler
must always enforce the law.   So Paul concluded that
God's laws must have penalties attached to them which
he could not justly omit.   Yet in forgiving man's sin God
was remitting the penalties.   How could he justly do so?
Paul's answer was ingenious.   The sacrifice of Christ,
who had incurred no penalty of sin, must have paid the
penalty for all mankind.   And this was possible because
the sinfulness of all mankind was ultimately due to the

original sin of Adam, which introduced the taint into originally perfect human nature. God had sent his Son to die as a propitiation for our sins " that he might be just, and the justifier of him which believeth in Jesus " (Rom. 3:26).

This legalistic theory of the atonement has always been a source of doubt and difficulty in Christian theology for it suffers from two serious ethical defects. We cannot shuffle off all the blame for our sin upon Adam; and in so far as our sin *is* due to a taint in our nature we should not be punished for what is not our fault. Second, it is not justice to allow an innocent person to accept the punishment of a guilty one, even if he volunteers to do so. The theory of an atonement through vicarious punishment of the innocent in place of the guilty is therefore morally unsound and must be rejected.

Fortunately, the whole theory is unnecessary. It is a false answer to a false problem. There is no analogy between the divine moral law and the law of the state. Man's laws and their penalties are mere human devices to force people to behave in certain ways that the civil authorities desire. The moral law of God is a natural law of the spiritual life of man. Its sanctions (or penalties) are not deliberately imposed to support the law but are the natural consequences of certain lines of action. The loving father, in the parable, can forgive his penitent prodigal son without demanding that the innocent elder brother pay any penalty. And God can forgive us the suffering we cause him through our sin without inflicting an undeserved punishment upon Jesus. But sins, though forgiven, still have their natural consequences.

God's problem is not to justify his loving desire to

forgive us, but to save us from the grip of sin. That sin is not the breaking of specific rules but the failure to keep on actively striving after higher and higher ideals. The consequences of this spiritual inertia (which is sin) are loss of the awareness of the presence of God within us as source of the moral law, failure to make any further progress in development of a higher spiritual life, the hardening of spiritual pride with consequent insensitivity to new problems and new opportunities, a growing tendency to excuse our own failures and thus slip backward to lower and lower moral levels as subtle temptations present themselves. And as sin spreads in society, society must morally stagnate and decay. God's problem is to keep the human race spiritually active, growing in grace and in the knowledge of God. The same problem is present at every level of the advance of civilization and culture, and at every stage in the moral progress of the individual. At the lower levels spiritual inertia is disturbed by the obvious effects of evil. At the higher levels nothing less than the knowledge of the life and death of Christ can solve the problem.

SALVATION FOR TIME AND ETERNITY

The salvation from sin that is thus wrought in human lives by the power of the gospel of Christ, and by the example of lesser servants of God, saves the individual from the effects of sin in this life and saves society from the cumulative effects of the sin of its members. The condition of the world today thus brings home to us how much we need the working of these religious forces among us.

But the salvation wrought in the individual is not only for time. It is for eternity. When spiritual inertia sets in, the soul ceases to grow and even begins to lose its gains. We have seen, in our earlier discussion of the structure and development of the soul, that what can be expected to survive bodily death is that part of our specific individuality which is concerned with those forms and expressions of beauty, goodness and truth that are independent of the physical life. We have seen, too, that the happiness of a soul depends upon the harmony of its developed individuality with the will to the greatest good — with God within. We thus see that the significance of salvation from sin is not merely temporal but eternal.

It is not the case that a soul which relapses into spiritual inertia is thereby eternally and completely lost, or that all those who do not come to the knowledge of Christ are eternally and completely lost. Such doctrines are monstrous. The beginnings of the development of the eternal part of a personality are wrought in it under the stimulus of the divine will within. Every normal human being in the course of his growth to maturity feels the operation of that higher will and comes under conviction of sin, even though he does not recognize the constraining influence within as divine. But he can cultivate the habit of ignoring its promptings — which is sin. The stronger this habit grows the more is the grip of sin fixed upon him. If it is not checked his spiritual development is eventually strangled. His personality grows out of harmony with the divine will. Such a personality we have no right to assume is eternally lost or eternally distorted and stunted. Reawakening and readjustment can take place in this life. There is good reason to suppose, therefore, that the same may be possible in the society that will exist hereafter. But that future life cannot but be the poorer for the opportunities of spiritual development which are lost in this.

THE RESURRECTION OF JESUS

Our examination of the function of Christ in history has shown us that his work was not completed by his life and teaching. It required also his death. But was it completed with his death? It is natural to say " Yes." But all the force of Christian history says " No." According to their own testimony — and we cannot doubt its honesty — his disciples relapsed into despair after the crucifixion. They believed it was the end of all their hopes. And then on the third day he appeared to them — to individuals and to groups. He enjoined them to go out and preach the things he had taught them, adding the promise of eternal life attested by his resurrection. The whole tenor of their story is that without this experience they would not have had the faith and courage to carry on. They made it the central feature of their preaching. Certainly something very remarkable happened to cause this change in their outlook and create this conviction that he had appeared to them. Was it merely a succession of hallucinations or was it something more?

One feature of the story which cannot be explained as a vision is that of the empty tomb. It is mentioned by all four Gospel writers, and Paul's references to the resurrection of the body show that he too believed it. We can discount a lot of the details, such as angelic appearances, as due to embellishment by rumor, for they are not without discrepancies. But the core of the story must be historical. On the morning of the third day, after observing the Sabbath in proper seclusion, a number of women went to the tomb and found it empty.   There is nothing incredible about this.   The women supposed at first that his enemies had had the body removed.   Anyone the least inclined to be skeptical will agree as to the probability. The priests would naturally want to dispose of it in some less honorable way, lest his disciples make the tomb a martyr's shrine and cause further trouble.   By the time the resurrection stories began to worry them the body would have been too far gone to produce as evidence.

Many critics of the stories believe that it was the empty tomb that led to the subsequent developments.   It suggested the idea of the resurrection, and dwelling on this idea produced hallucinations which were later embellished in the Easter stories.

But even when one has made all due allowance for the easy growth of rumor and embellishment, even among honest witnesses, it is not easy to dismiss these stories as based on mere hallucination.   There was no atmosphere of expectation in the disciples' minds such as is necessary to produce hallucinations, no wild excitement in their meetings such as is required for a whole group to become subject to the same hallucination at the same time.

There is no reasonable historical doubt that the apostles *believed* they had seen him, together, as a group, on two occasions after his death, that a great crowd of several hundreds believed they saw him on another occasion, and that several individuals believed he had appeared to them privately.   Paul's statement in I Corinthians 15 is sufficient in itself to prove this, for the authenticity of this letter and the reliability of Paul's witness are recognized by scholars as beyond question.   Coupled with the stories in the Gospels and the subsequent history of

the movement, which shows the tremendous conviction
with which they preached the resurrection, one fact is
placed beyond doubt — these individuals and groups of
people certainly had visual (and probably auditory) experiences which convinced them thoroughly that Jesus
had in some way risen from the dead.

It was natural and inevitable for those who had these
experiences to believe they had seen a miracle. It was
an age in which almost everybody believed in miracles.
The ministry of Jesus had been marked by many remarkable cases of healing. These we can understand as due
to psychological causes. But the psychological explanation was not understood in those days and the witnesses
could not help believing that Jesus somehow possessed
miraculous powers. Rumor, of course, exaggerated the
stories with additions that are psychologically and physically impossible. So the followers of Jesus, believing that
miracles had happened before in the life of Jesus, believed another and greater miracle had happened when
they had the strange experience of his visual appearance
before them. Coupled with the disappearance of the
body from the tomb it made them believe he had been
physically raised from the dead — although he appeared
and disappeared in a way no physical body could do.

The belief in a physical miracle must, however, be
rejected. If it were possible for God to work such miracles it would place on him the whole responsibility for
allowing physical disease and suffering to continue in
the world. Further, all our scientific knowledge unites
to reject the notion that mind can interfere to this extent with physical nature.

Yet, as already shown, the evidence seems too strong
to dismiss these appearances as mere hallucinations. So

we are driven to ask whether they could in some way be real without being miraculous. Here we must face phenomena that are on the border line of human knowledge. The Society for Psychical Research has for many years been investigating cases of this sort with inconclusive results. They have exposed much fraud and found much honest error and self-deception; but there is a residue of evidence which convinces many capable investigators that the power of one mind to influence another, and even affect its sensory experience, is not limited to the ordinary channels of communication. Psychologists at Duke University have gathered a great deal of experimental evidence confirming this view, though others have performed similar experiments with negative results. It seems to be only in conditions of exceptional strain and excitement that normal minds become so shaken out of their habitual modes of operation as to exercise this influence upon others with any great strength or clarity. With somewhat abnormal minds it appears to be commoner, but still is rare and spasmodic, difficult to demonstrate experimentally and to control.

It must be admitted that the evidence is as yet inconclusive. But the prevailing skepticism seems to be due to philosophical prejudice rather than to empirical tests. We have seen reason in earlier chapters to believe in the survival of the mind after the death of the body. If it is possible, therefore, for one mind to influence the experience of another mind directly, then the risen soul of Jesus may have given the Easter experiences to his disciples without the miracle of a risen body. The essential point in the resurrection stories would then be true. We should have to regard the belief in the physical resurrection as merely an unfortunate addition due to the

removal of the body from the tomb. If the disciples had
gone forth to preach that the spirit of Jesus, rather than
the body, had appeared to them they would have found
many more people ready to believe them, both in the
Greco-Roman world and in the world of the present day.

The most important objection to this explanation of
the appearances is that we do not have other well authen-
ticated cases of the same thing. If Jesus could appear to
his loved ones after his death why do not others do so?
The only answer to this is that Jesus was a most exceptional person and it may well be that he succeeded in
doing what the souls of others have not the power of will
to carry through. Even though the mind survives the
shock of bodily death it must be very much shaken and
temporarily incomplete. Mind is a system of interests
and our interests are so much involved with the body as
their means of expression, so much wrapped up with
lowly and temporal desires, that we cannot but anticipate
the necessity for a considerable period of adjustment before we again become capable of decisive action. And
the fact that the dead do not normally communicate with
us would indicate that in the adjustment the capacity for
direct influence on earthly minds is normally lost. If
the risen Jesus really succeeded in impressing upon his
followers such a vivid experience of his presence as they
undoubtedly had it is just one further indication of the
power of his will to free itself from the concerns of the
flesh and devote itself to the good of those he loved.

This explanation of the central doctrine of historic
Christianity cannot be regarded as proved. No form
of resurrection doctrine is sufficiently well established to
be put into a creed and made a test of religious fellowship. The power of Christ to save from sin does not re-

quire belief in the resurrection of his body. But the
theory here advanced seems to be the most reasonable
explanation of the historical record. And the doctrine
of the risen Lord is one that has proved its value in the
life of the church. In the form here given it may therefore be accepted as part of a rational faith, helping to con-
firm that hope of eternity which rounds out the meaning
of our life and gives us courage to face its darkest phases.

Must Religion Be Institutionalized?

FUNCTIONS AND FAULTS OF INSTITUTIONS

INSTITUTIONS are the recognized forms of orderly social relations, the instruments of group action. A community or association of people without institutions would be an unorganized crowd. But this ordering of our lives by institutions is always somewhat galling and restrictive of our freedom. An institution is like the yoke that is put across a span of oxen. It is the means whereby they tug their load and work together in a common service, but it is burdensome and binding and apt to gall their shoulders. Or, to change the figure slightly, an institution is like the yoke used by water-carriers to fit across their shoulders and hang a bucket at either end. It gives them power to lift a heavier load, but it restricts the freedom of their arms and presses painfully where it does not perfectly fit.

Need our religion be a yoke upon us? The religious life is a tender plant, a growth within the innermost recesses of the soul. Must it submit to external regulation? Need it conform to the instruments of public action? Can it not be cherished and cultivated in the privacy of the inner life and express itself in the freedom of the individual without incurring the restrictions and dangers of institutionalization? Institutions create vested interests. They hamper freedom of thought and expression. They press us into a common mold and gall the exceptional individual by their failure to fit his special needs. Religious institutions manifest these evils no less than others. Cannot religion be one area of life left free from the burden of them?

We must admit the truth of these charges. But still the plea for freedom from institutionalization of religion must be denied. The central lesson of religion is that "no man liveth to himself." Least of any phase of our lives can religion be cut off from society. Its most fundamental root is the inner demand that we concern ourselves with the good of others. And there is little good that we can do alone. Our religious faith is the most precious thing that we possess and we cannot will another's good and keep it from him. To spread the faith and carry out its program of good will we must work with others. And there can be no cooperative social action without those recognized forms and instrumentalities which we call institutions.

Yet religion can be, and commonly is, overinstitutionalized. Without constant vigilance and critical self-appraisement its institutions become distorted and burdened by the vested interests of officeholders, rigid and ill-adapted to new knowledge and new conditions, inefficient and restrictive. Jesus came to preach to a people whose religion was heavily overinstitutionalized, burdened with the vested interests of priests, distorted by crude and outworn ceremonies. He cleansed the temple of the money changers and sellers of sacrificial animals, repudiated the senseless prohibitions on various foods ("Not that which goeth into the mouth defileth a man; but that which cometh out" [Matt. 15:11]) , and preached a simple religion of faith and love. His followers were to have a religion that should not be a burden — should not be overinstitutionalized. " Come unto me, all ye that labor and are heavy laden, and I will give you rest. Take my yoke upon you, and learn of me; for I am meek and lowly in heart: and ye shall find rest unto your souls " (Matt. 11:28–29).

Yet he did not leave his followers as a group devoid of institutions to bind them together and express their faith. From the beginning of his ministry he endorsed the act of baptism as a symbol of repentance and adoption of the " gospel " he preached. And on his last night with his disciples he instituted the communion supper as a memorial and symbol of fellowship. Apart from these practices he set up no formal system of worship, but he taught his followers to pray, joined with them in reading scriptures and singing hymns, and sent them forth to preach. He established no officialdom, but left to his followers the task of organizing the church. The authority he is alleged by Catholic writers to have conferred upon Peter (Matt. 16:18–19) was not intended for Peter alone, for in precisely the same words it is said (Matt. 18:17–18) to be the function of any particular local church. The plain inference is that he left to his followers the task of developing their own church organization in whatever form they found most efficient.

Christ, therefore, sought to leave behind him a religious society, not devoid of institutions, but cherishing those he gave them and developing others as they were found to be necessary or useful, without allowing any institution to become burdensome. Even " the sabbath," he said, " was made for man, and not man for the sabbath " (Mark 2:27). The test of Christian institutions, as developed and practiced by the church, must therefore be their value for Christian life and work. The institu-

tions established by Jesus himself should be practiced in
the same spirit, and in a form which preserves the same
symbolism, as he gave to them.   But it is not in accord
with the spirit of Christ to create bitterness and division
by insisting on detailed agreement in the observation of
ceremonies.   We should remember the Pauline injunction, " The letter killeth, but the spirit giveth life"
(II Cor. 3:6) .

THE UNITY OF THE CHURCH

All who recognize the central place of Jesus Christ in
the revelation of God in history, by that very fact form
one body.   This is not merely a historical and mystical
dogma.   It is an inevitable psychological necessity.   A
psychological group is created by the recognition of a
common leadership.   The whole Christian church, therefore, forms one spiritual body, of which Christ is the head
and functional center.   There are disorders and lesions
(or breaks) within that body, but these cannot destroy its
essential spiritual unity.   Yet these disorders and lesions
cripple its power and destroy its influence.   The hope of
human society lies in the development by the church of
a set of institutions which can become effective instruments of its underlying unity of spirit while remaining
sufficiently flexible to express that spirit in all its multi-
farious forms.

The great mistake of the church in the past has been
an exaggeration of the importance of agreement in matters of belief and ceremonial form.   Very early in the
history of the church, when teachings arose which the
majority felt were false, they thought it necessary, in defense of the truth, to thrust the false teachers and their
followers out from their fellowship.   Yet all human his-

tory shows that the best defense of the truth is freedom
of discussion in an atmosphere of mutual respect and
love.   The churches should cease to make their creeds
tests of fellowship.   At most, creeds should be brief state-
ments of general belief for the guidance of inquirers, and
constantly subject to reformulation.   It is impossible
for a man to coerce his mind to believe what does not
appear to him consistent with fact and logically reasonable.   But any person who is sufficiently at one with the
spirit of Christ to wish to work and fellowship in common cause with those who find in him the supreme revelation of God in history is, in spirit, a member of the body
of Christ and should not be turned away.

Such a person, even though he has intellectual difficulty in believing that God is a superhuman personal
being, still should be admitted.   God is in him and has
joined him to Christ, even though he cannot believe that
the psychological force which does this is part of a conscious power transcending all human nature.   Fortunately it is only a very few of those who really desire to
honor and serve Christ as their spiritual leader who cannot follow him in belief in a personal and superhuman
God.   And unfortunately those with these intellectual
difficulties are usually restrained by them from seeking
full fellowship with the Christian church.   If the church
should open its doors to these " humanists," as they often
call themselves, it will not be swamped or adversely in-
fluenced by them.   For humanism is an emasculated
form of religious belief.   It lacks vitality and the power
to weather crises.   It is a half-way stage in which few
people are likely to remain long.   And those who enter
upon it are more likely to come out on the side of a full
Christian faith if spiritually nourished in the fellowship

of the church than if thrust out to form some small fellowship of their own.

But if the church is to provide a spiritual home and sphere of religious service for all types of human minds it must allow different congregations to develop different institutional forms for their work and worship. Differences of temperament, tradition, education and individuality create differences of personality which cannot find adequate help and expression in the same way. Further, groups of people with special interests and distinctive beliefs and ideas should be free to organize distinct congregations for their cultivation and propagation. The measure of disunity thus developed is the inevitable counterpart of that freedom of conscience and freedom of thought in the search for truth which is so vital to the religious life. Fortunately, most denominations of Christendom have already learned to make room for these special varieties of religious thought and experience.

In cities it is comparatively easy for almost any person to find a congregation with which he can work and worship in mutual helpfulness. But in small towns and country areas it is often difficult. Here there is great need for the spirit of Christian charity and mutual accommodation. Each individual should recognize that the creation of an efficient instrument of religious service to the community is more important than the cultivation of the preferred practices, and propagation of the special ideas, of any small group. If freedom of conscience be granted on matters of belief and individual practice, then, for those religious institutions in which the practice of the congregation must needs be uniform, the principle of majority rule would seem to be in accord with the spirit of Christ. We can put our trust in the hope that, with such freedom of conscience and belief, truth and the higher values will in the long run prevail. Meantime the community as a whole would be receiving the sort of religious service that the majority felt best suited to their needs.

The same trust, that truth and the higher values will prevail where freedom is allowed, should enable us also to adopt the principle of majority rule as a solution of the problem of creating institutions to serve the larger functions of the church, beyond those of the local congregation. Home and foreign missions, social action, the training of the ministry, services of advice, aid and oversight, and other matters, require an organization of the church on a much larger scale than that of the local congregation. At present our exaggerated emphasis upon differences of creed and institution has created a disastrous state of division in this area of the church's life. We are organized and divided into a multitude of denominations, and our denominational institutions have become vested interests that tend to perpetuate the spirit of disunity.

The combination of individual and congregational freedom with democratic majority rule for the larger cooperative enterprises of the church could probably be successfully worked out were it not hindered by the dogma of specific historical revelations, giving alleged authoritative form to creedal beliefs and institutions. If there are specific, divinely given instructions in the Bible as to what Christians must believe about God, Christ and man, and how they must organize the church and conduct its worship, then where there is conflict of opinion and practice one or more of the conflicting parties is not merely less wise than the other, but is positively wrong. No party feels that it can compromise on something which it believes to be specifically ordained by divine revelation. Thus all Christians who hold the dogma of specific revealed ideas feel they must stand rigidly for their principles.

Those, on the other hand, who reject this dogma of specific revealed ideas find it much easier to come to agreement on what constitute the best institutional forms for the life of the church. These liberal-minded leaders in nearly all the denominations of Christendom are gradually drawing their divided groups together into closer and closer cooperation. And as the dogma of specific revelation fades into oblivion we can expect to see the unity, freedom and power of the church increase. We probably shall not see precisely the same form of government adopted in every area, nor a precise similarity of other institutions in any area; but we shall see a development of that unity amid difference whereby alone social organizations can combine freedom with efficiency.

THE CHURCH AND SECULAR INSTITUTIONS

The need for institutions and for unity receives special emphasis when we consider the function of the church in relation to political and economic institutions. Human welfare and human sin are inextricably wrapped up with the secular institutions of society. And religious ideas can make little impact upon these secular institutions until they themselves take on institutional form.

Jesus did not concern himself directly with the political and economic institutions of his day. It was beyond his power and that of his followers at the time to make any impact upon them. And he wisely taught no theory as to how they should be organized if and when his followers had the power. For no one type of organization of political and economic life is suitable for every people in every stage of development. Christian ethics in these spheres can only set up the guiding principle of the Golden Rule, the greatest good of all concerned. Jesus turned his back upon the futile and dangerous political movements of his day which set themselves in opposition to the tyrannous but comparatively orderly and efficient government of Rome. He endorsed the institution of the state in principle by telling his hearers to " render unto Caesar the things that are Caesar's " (Mark 12:17). But he also established a new institution, which he called " the kingdom of heaven," which was to work gradually in its contact with secular society until, like the yeast in a batch of dough, it should at length transform the whole lump. This is the meaning of the parable of the leaven (Matt. 13:33). And the " kingdom of heaven " is another name for the Christian society, the " body of Christ " (I Cor. 12:27).

Jesus' mission on earth was the saving of men from sin. His instrument was the " kingdom of heaven," which takes an organized form as the Christian church. His first task was to establish that instrument. But he clearly recognized that in performing its task the church could not help but influence, and must undertake to transform, the institutions of secular society. As soon as the church attained a position of influence in the Roman state it proceeded to attempt this. The chief of its triumphs were the abolition of the gladiatorial games, the securing of some improvements in the treatment of slaves, the introduction of some elementary provision for the poor, and the elevation of the conception of marriage. But

Christianity began to exercise influence in the Roman state only when that state was already crumbling before the barbarian invasion. The Dark Ages came upon Europe and the Greco-Roman-Christian culture was almost lost beneath the avalanche.

Three great things the church strove to do for secular society in the period that followed, two of which were entirely good and the third a well intentioned but badly executed failure. The church kept alight the lamp of learning in its monasteries. It established great institutions for the care of the poor and needy. It made a bold attempt to secure the political unity and peace of Europe in the only way that at the time seemed possible, by getting the unruly kings and feudal lords to accept the ultimate authority of the pope in the political system of Christendom. But the opposition was too strong, and the church itself too corrupt, to carry through this grandiose, mistaken, but originally well intentioned scheme. The resistance to it gave political support to the rise of Protestantism. And Protestantism, in reaction from the papal effort to secure temporal power, either subjected the church to the state or decreed their complete separation. Thus Protestantism at the beginning conceived the task of the church as that of saving individual souls, leaving to the state the shaping of secular institutions.

But more and more in recent decades Christians of all denominations have awakened to the fact that the sin and suffering of the individual are due in large part to the institutions of our political and economic life. The task of saving souls from sin and doing good to our fellow man is wrapped up with that of reshaping some of our institutions. Economic conditions create slums, raise children in disease and ignorance, enforce poverty in the midst of plenty, encourage trickery in business and the hoarding of wealth to gratify pride and the lust for power. And these things generate sin and suffering faster than Christian truth and charity can overcome them. The Christian principles of love and justice demand that these conditions shall be changed. And our religious institutions must be fashioned and used in a way that will meet this challenge.

There are many movements within the church today which show that it is awake to this need. The great difficulty felt by Christian leaders is to know what to do. Ministers of religion are not experts on economics and other problems of state; and good will is futile without knowledge. It may even cause harm.

Here there are two broad principles to guide us. First, where the issue is clear, the need and the remedy apparent but only the will to apply it lacking, there the church should cast its full weight in support of the reform. Second, where there is real doubt as to the right means to cure an evil, there the church should be active in demanding that a cure be found. Vested interests will tolerate evils and claim that nothing can be done. Cures can be found only by thought and experiment. If the community is not fully aware of the extent of an evil it will tolerate the " do nothing, try nothing " policy of vested interests. The church should be the most sensitive part of the community's social conscience, discovering the things that are wrong, pointing out the evils, and crying aloud that a remedy be found. Only thus can the wheels of democratic machinery be moved to mend the wrongs of those who are too feeble to exert enough pressure to secure a remedy for themselves.

INSTITUTIONS AND THE THEORY OF HUMAN NATURE

In regard to both religious and secular institutions we find a tendency for people to adopt one or other of two types of thought, liberal or conservative. Liberals are ready to make changes and to give increased freedom to individuals and groups. Conservatives are loath to make changes or remove restrictions. The motives for these attitudes, of course, are mixed. In part the motive is self-interest. Those who profit by the existing situation want to maintain it, while those whose advancement is hampered by it want to change it. In part the motive is restlessness and love of variety on the one hand, and inertia and fondness for familiar ways on the other.

But the most important motive goes deeper. The conservative has a relatively low view of human nature. He does not want change because he fears the results. He wants to keep up restrictions because he believes increased liberty will be abused. The liberal, on the other hand, has a relatively high view of human nature. He trusts his fellow men and is ready to enlarge their liberties. The blame for existing evils he places on existing institutions rather than on human beings and so he wants to change the institutions.

Now any frank review of history will show that both sides have made mistakes. Disorder, chaos and war may come through unwise change or the failure to maintain necessary restrictions. But progress is impossible unless we are willing to make experimental changes and take some risks in enlargement of liberties. The balance of power usually lies with those who wish to maintain existing institutions with their present restrictions; and the strong selfish motivation of vested interests supports the

doubts and fears of the conservatives. Society is therefore much more inclined to err on the side of conserva-
tism than on that of liberalism. Hence, if progress is to
be made, we need to strengthen the liberal philosophy of
human nature, the philosophy that trusts human nature
enough to seek to expand human freedom and experimentally change our institutions to seek improvement.
At the same time this liberal philosophy must be sufficiently realistic to avoid serious errors and be alert to
rectify mistakes.

It is an interesting study to observe how various phi-
losophies of human nature have affected the attitude to
the state and the church of those who held them. Plato,
at the time he wrote the *Republic,* believed the ordinary
man to be quite incapable of a true insight into right
and wrong. That was possible only for the philosopher.
Therefore the ideal state must be governed by a specially
trained philosopher king, and the common people must
be deprived of all political power. The Stoics believed
that the human mind partakes of a universal reason
which runs through all things. They therefore advo-
cated the abolition of all distinctions of class and race and
persuaded some of the early Roman emperors to amelio-
rate the condition of slaves and extend Roman citizen-
ship to the subject peoples.

St. Augustine believed that man is a fallen creature incapable of any real good unless specially redeemed by
God. He therefore despaired of human institutions and
urged the strengthening of the central authority of the
pope and the bishops within the church. Martin Luther
adopted Augustine's view of man, but believed that the
spirit of God would enlighten the mind of the Christian
to understand the scriptures. He therefore rejected au-

thoritarianism within the church but supported a conservative and authoritarian policy in the state.

Thomas Hobbes believed that man is motivated only by selfish drives to his own satisfactions. He therefore argued that all power in church and state must be vested absolutely in a single sovereign authority. Later generations of British moralists, such as Locke, Shaftesbury, Butler, Adam Smith and John Stuart Mill, utterly rejected Hobbes and taught an optimistic view of human nature which has greatly assisted the development of Anglo-American liberalism and democracy in church and state. This optimism has even gone so far as to blind many people to the evils inherent in the industrial system and the danger of militarism in certain states that have not yet outgrown their feudalism. Karl Marx, on the other hand, believed that economic motives are the real drives that shape the course of history. He therefore refused to believe that a just distribution of wealth could be obtained without violence and taught the doctrine of the class war.

The analysis of human nature developed in this book gives us a balanced and yet hopeful view. We have seen that it is inevitable that the early development of personality in every child is egoistic and that the main force of habit consists of these infantile egoisms and the narrow social interests inculcated by the narrow social groups (family, class, race, nation, etc.) with which the individual is associated in his growing years. We must therefore recognize that we will always have to reckon with the forces of selfishness and special group interests. Further, we have seen that, even at a high level of character development, these habits can stifle further spiritual aspirations, especially when they take the form of a pride of the individual in his own moral achievements. But we have also seen that God is in every man as a will to the good of all which condemns the individual's selfishness and narrowness whenever he can be brought to think clearly enough.

We thus see that, though individuals may become impervious to the moral demand within, the group as a whole cannot. There will always be some sensitive souls among the adults to whom an appeal can be made on higher moral grounds. Further, there will always be a period in the life of the youth of each generation when the will to the good of all breaks through their infantile egoisms and the group prejudices and adult selfishness are not yet set hard. At this period youth responds to idealism. Thus each new generation may be brought to set before itself higher and more generous goals, broader freedom and greater respect for the dignity of man.

It is thus that progress has been made in the past. And there is no reason why progress should not go on. Temporary reactions there may be, such as have occurred in the last forty years. It is even possible that a great civilization may stagnate and decline. But reaction and decline are not inevitable. Neither is progress. There is a battle to be fought against inertia and reaction. But with wisdom, zeal and faith it can be won. Indeed, because God is in men, it can never be finally lost.

THE CHURCH AND WAR

What shall we say of the relation of the church to the terrible secular institution of war? Can the church ever rightly give its moral support to the state in the conduct of war? Many Christians, remembering the injunction to " love your enemies," and thinking of the horrors of wholesale slaughter, have emphatically concluded that it cannot. They make the mistake, however, either of setting up the principle, " Thou shalt not kill," as a specific absolute to which no exception can ever be allowed, or of thinking that the greatest evil that can befall any man is to lose his life. But both ideas are false. To love our neighbors and our enemies is to do to all the greatest possible good. If that involves killing, then, at whatever risk to ourselves, we must be prepared to kill. And Jesus clearly recognized that this might be necessary: " But whoso shall offend one of these little ones which believe in me, it were better for him that a millstone were hanged about his neck, and that he were drowned in the depth of the sea " (Matt. 18:6) .

There can be no law without a readiness to use force to uphold it. And the law cannot be upheld by force unless the servants of the state are ready to take life if necessary. The primary function of the state is to protect the community in life and limb and in possession of its means of livelihood. Jesus was not preaching anarchy when he urged his hearers to be ready to turn the other cheek rather than offer resistance to unjust attack. He was talking to people who lived under the law and urging that they should avoid all attempt at private vengeance. His " doctrine of nonresistance " presupposes the existence of the state to protect the innocent and restrain the violent. He did not mean that if any king or governor should become a disciple of his he should refuse any longer to carry out the primary duty of his office — to protect his people from armed violence arising from within the state or from without.

The state then must perform its function of internal justice and external defense. And the church must give it moral support in the performance of those duties. It is tremendously important, however, that the church should critically scrutinize the conduct of the state in the performance of all its functions — most of all the terrible duty of war. It must demand that all the dealings of the state with other states be made public as soon as possible, so that moral judgment can be pronounced upon them. It must demand justice and good will in international relations. It must demand cooperation of all states in the maintenance of peace, the protection of the weak, the upholding of international justice, law and order. And the church in each state must demand that its own state be ready to use force where necessary, or combine in the use of an international force, to help any neighbor state to perform that essential function for which the state exists — to protect its people from armed attack on their lives and means of livelihood, whether from tyranny within or from aggressors from without. This is the only true application of the principle of love to neighbors on the level of international relations.

THE NEED OF PRIVATE DEVOTIONS

We cannot, then, escape the institutionalization of religion. Religion needs institutions because it has a function to perform in relation to the institutions of society; also because it involves social relations, and institutions are the ordering principles of all society. We can do our best to improve our religious and secular institutions, but, because human beings are so different, they cannot be made perfectly fitting for all. Our social relations, both secular and religious, must therefore always occasionally gall us. Man cannot always find rest and solace for his soul in his fellow man. It is then that there arises most poignantly our need for the other side of the religious life, beyond the institutional and social — the life of private devotion, meditation and prayer.

But the spirit must have practice in the art of private devotion if it is to avail us in our times of need.   Both public and private devotions are a spiritual preparation for the problems and crises of practical life.   But private prayer is also a refuge and source of strength in the very midst of the crisis, if we are accustomed to its practice.   Prayer is communion with God, a talking over our problems with him.   In prayer we come face to face with God, for God is within us.   We become sensitive to the nature and purpose of His will and find guidance from Him.   We reintegrate our torn and divided selves with Him and find peace, strength and calm.

It is a good thing to make our desires known to God in petition.   We can there and then examine them in His presence and reject those that are unworthy.   But it is a terrible mistake to regard prayer as a means of getting God to do for us what we can and ought to do for ourselves.   It is also a bad mistake to regard prayer as a means of getting God on our side.   Prayer is rather a means of getting ourselves on His side.

The question of what we may rightly expect from God in answer to prayer is not an easy one to answer.   Spiritual help we certainly can and do receive.   But can we pray for God's influence on others or for physical blessings?   Here we must remember what we have already learned to recognize as the limits of God's opportunity to intervene in the course of nature on our behalf.   Much harm is done by religious teachers in creating expectations of answers to prayer that cannot be fulfilled.

If we examine the model prayer given by Jesus to his

disciples we find that it contains only one request for a physical good, and that for merely the essential basis of the physical life — " Give us this day our daily bread." And this is a prayer which he and his hearers would expect to be answered through God's influence on *human* activity. The same applies to the one other occasion on which he prayed concerning a physical need — the prayer for escape from his persecutors. And this contains the significant phrase that recognizes limitations to what God can do, even in his influence on human beings: " Father, *if it be possible,* let this cup pass from me " (Matt. 26:39).

From the practice of Jesus we therefore get little encouragement to engage in prayers for physical benefits, but much encouragement in the practice of prayer for its spiritual value. Jesus apparently believed (and there seems no reason why we also should not believe) that God may have ways unknown to us of influencing human behavior in answer to our prayers — though he recognized that this power must have its limitations. In the same tentative and humble spirit of his " Father, if it be possible " we may well pray for God to exert his influence upon ourselves and others. And this may include prayer for those spiritual influences which can help in the healing of the body. We do not know the limits of the power of prayer in these things and so we must pray in faith. But the prayer of faith does not mean a belief that God can and will fulfill our wishes, even if what we wish is purely good. It means rather the faith that God will work with us in the effort to produce the good and that, even though the goal be something we cannot attain and he cannot give us, yet the effort thus to work with God, in itself, is abundantly worth while.

CONCLUSION

This book has sought to interpret the religious experience of mankind in harmony with our knowledge of science and history. It has sought to show man's need of God and his need of religious truth. The task of interpretation must be done again and again in the light of new religious experience and new scientific and historical knowledge. And many minds must work over the same facts, checking the interpretations. We must expect some hesitation and disagreement in detail. But from the analysis of all the material at our disposal there emerge two great complementary truths, which form the central thesis of this interpretation and which are abundantly supported by the evidence. The first is affirmative: The one true God is revealed in every man as a will that demands of him that he seek the greatest good of all. The second is negative: We have no right to assert that any man has any revelation of the will of God, other than that which he receives through this operation of the will of God within him and other men.

It is from the denial of one or other of these two truths that nearly all our religious troubles arise. From the denial of the first proceed irreligion, agnosticism and secularism. From the denial of the second proceed unjustified dogmatism, most of our sectarianism, and a great deal of the blindness to the first great truth, with its evil results. From the acceptance of the first truth arise faith in the reality of a God of love, within us and above us, and assurance of the knowledge of his will for our lives. From the acceptance of the second arise liberty and tolerance, the mind that is open to new truth and the clear recognition as to where it is to be found — i.e., in our religious and moral experience as we walk with God, in the insights of others who have walked still more closely with him, and through the testing of all our conclusions in the light of science and history.

It has been the aim of this book, first to establish these two great truths, next to use the method thus indicated to inquire into further truth. In this process we have found it necessary to reject as error some features of traditional Christian belief. But we have also found a great central body of that belief which can be accepted as sound and true. We have added nothing new except as recent science and discovery have cast new light on old truths; and most of the changes of thought thus introduced have merely been changes of emphasis. But the results are such as to give us new confidence in that mode of religious life and thought which we owe to Jesus Christ. That religion has established a great tradition of which we can rejoice to be a part. The evils Christianity has wrought are due to errors that are not essential to it. The great body of truth that remains is the power responsible for the enormous good it has done. The essential thought and practice of the religion of Jesus Christ must remain forever the hope of the world.

Index